Motor Cycles

Also available in the Questions and Answers series:

Automobile Engines

Diesel Engines

Automobile Electrical Systems

Automobile Transmission Systems

Electric Motors

QUESTIONS & ANSWERS

Motor Cycles

G. Forsdyke

Newnes Technical Books

THE BUTTERWORTH GROUP

UNITED KINGDOM
Butterworth & Co. (Publishers) Ltd
London: 88 Kingsway, WC2B 6AB

AUSTRALIA
Butterworths Pty Ltd
Sydney: 586 Pacific Highway, NSW 2067
also at Melbourne, Brisbane, Adelaide and Perth

CANADA
Butterworth & Co. (Canada) Ltd
Toronto: 2265 Midland Avenue, Scarborough, Ontario M1P 4S1

NEW ZEALAND
Butterworths of New Zealand Ltd
Wellington: 26-28 Waring Taylor Street, 1

SOUTH AFRICA
Butterworth & Co. (South Africa) (Pty) Ltd
Durban: 152-154 Gale Street

USA
Butterworth (Publishers) Inc
Boston: 19 Cummings Park, Woburn, Mass. 01801

First published in 1976 by Newnes Technical Books,
a Butterworth imprint

© Butterworth & Co (Publishers) Ltd, 1976

All rights reserved. No part of this publication may be reproduced
or transmitted in any form or by any means, including photocopying
and recording, without the written permission of the copyright
holder, application for which should be addressed to the publishers.
Such written permission must also be obtained before any part of
this publication is stored in a retrieval system of any nature.

This book is sold subject to the Standard Conditions of Sale of
Net Books and may not be sold in the UK below the net price
given by the publishers in their current price list.

ISBN 0 408 00232 8

Typeset by Butterworths LPD
Printed and bound in England by Butler & Tanner Ltd,
Frome and London

CONTENTS

1
Types of Machine 1

2
Engines 11

3
Carburation 23

4
Ignition Systems 39

5
Gearboxes 47

6
Motor Cycle Parts 56

7
Electrical Systems 69

8
Routine Maintenance 72

9
Licensing, Insurance, Legal Notes 90

10
On the Road 96

Index 111

PREFACE

As an instructor at motor-cycle maintenance classes, I have long been aware of the need for a book setting out the questions most asked by the amateur motor cyclist and the answers necessary to give the rider sufficient knowledge not only to purchase a machine but also with which to keep it in a roadworthy condition. Today, buying a motor cycle involves the outlay of a considerable amount of money and if the machine is to give value for that money it must be suitable for the work it has to do and go on doing that work with a minimum amount of visits to the professional repair shop.

This book fills the purpose of introducing the reader to the vast and evergrowing choice in the initial selection of a motor cycle, whether it be a 50cc moped for ride-to-work runs or a full-blooded sports model for high speed touring. It then goes into detail about how the machinery works and considerable space is given to detailing a regular maintenance schedule aimed at obviating the chances of a roadside breakdown.

The advantages and disadvantages of various accessories are dealt with and the question of choice of clothing is gone into in some detail. In all, this is a book for the motor cyclist who does not want to make mistakes and it is capable of giving a good grounding to the novice rider as well as of being a useful reference work to the slightly more experienced rider.

G.F.

1
TYPES OF MACHINE

What types of machine are available?

With the Japanese move into motor-cycle production in the biggest possible way in the early 1960s, there is now a greater range of motor cycles and mopeds available than ever before.

The choice is enormous. There are single-gear mopeds capable of less than 48 km/h (30 mph) but with fantastic petrol economy, a range of lightweight machines still offering good economy but with the facility of travelling a further distance without discomfort to machine or rider, long-range touring machines, and complex multi-cylinder, high-speed models aimed purely at the fast-riding enthusiast.

In what capacity sizes are true motor cycles produced?

Machines are currently available from under 50 cc to 1300 cc. The small 50s are basically commuter models and those in the 125 cc range can be used for commuting, and even serious touring. Machines of 650 cc and upwards tend to be sports tourers.

Is there a wide range of choice in each capacity class of motor cycle?

There are a wide variety of machines offered by many different manufacturers in practically every capacity class and also in many intermediate classes.

The recognised capacity classes are 50, 75, 100, 125, 250, 350, 500, 750, 1000 cc, but recently manufacturers, particularly the Japanese, have introduced odd-sized machines, often to take advantage of particular insurance rates available in various countries.

Is there a choice of two-stroke and four-stroke in all capacity classes?

Thanks to Honda, whose entire enormous range - except for four competition machines - consists of four strokes, there is a choice between two-stroke and four-stroke machines for practically every capacity size up to 750 cc.

There are only two 750 cc two-stroke machines - a three-cylinder Suzuki with water cooling and a three-cylinder Kawasaki. In the 1000 cc class the choice is limited to four strokes with 1000 cc machines being offered by the Italian Laverda, the Japanese Kawaski and the German BMW.

What capacity sizes are available in mopeds?

Most moped manufacturers produce machines of only 50 cc which, whilst keeping them within the law, result in a machine of maximum available power.

How does a moped differ from a motor cycle?

By legal definition a moped is a powered two-wheel machine with an engine capacity of less than 50 cc which is also capable of being propelled by means of pedals.

In terms of the engine-size limitations mopeds have, generally speaking, lower-power outputs than motor cycles. But manufacturers, given the legal limits on riding age - a youngster may ride a moped before he is allowed to own a motor cycle - have produced a range of super-fast mopeds which, in some cases, have considerably more power than some of the smaller, commuter motor cycles.

Does the fact that a moped is fitted with pedals mean that these have to be used for getting the machine under way and for helping it up hills?

Such is the state of motor-cycle engine design today that pedals on many mopeds are added purely to comply with the law. Once the machine has been started - a pedal is usually used for this - only on freak gradients are the pedals necessary on the more powerful machine.

What are the advantages of mopeds over motor cycles?

In many countries moped riders do not have to pass any form of driving test at all. Some countries have less rigorous procedures than for full-size motor cycles or cars - in Britain, for example, a man having passed a car-driving test does not need to take a separate examination for the moped two-wheeler.

The utilitarian mopeds are bought with economy in mind, both during initial purchase and regular running.

Are all mopeds of simple, single-gear design?

Mopeds, enjoying their current popularity, come in a large variety of transmission types. There are simple, single-gear machines, models with constantly variable transmission and others with hand clutch and multi-speed gearboxes.

Are all mopeds of four-stroke design?

The vast majority of mopeds use two-stroke engines when the fuel has to be pre-mixed with oil or obtained from a special dispenser. One or two companies, notably Honda, produce four-stroke mopeds but the extra cost of the four-stroke engine, on an ultra-low price model, favours the simpler two-stroke power unit.

What sort of fuel economy can one expect from a moped?

The most basic mopeds should return 1000 km/litre (or 150 miles/UK gal*) if driven with due care. Some approach 1500 km/litre (190 miles/UK gal) but some of the super-sports versions which are little more than near-racing machines can achieve only 370 km/litre (80 miles/UK gal).

How should a prospective purchaser select a machine?

The choice of machines available is so wide that the first consideration should be a careful analysis of what the motor cycle or moped will be required to do.

A decision should be made as to whether the machine will be used solely as a ride-to-work transport covering perhaps only 8 km (5 miles) a day in which case there will be little advantage in selecting anything but a moped.

If riding is to be confined to commuting within heavily built-up areas with constant traffic congestion then there is little point in buying a machine over 250 cc. Motor cycles of 125 cc are generally held to be the ideal machine for traffic threading and manoeuverability in congested areas.

For the owner who wishes to add the occasional 20 or 40 kilometre (12½ or 25 miles) jaunt to his programme perhaps a moped with more luxury equipment such as rear springing is called for.

The small-capacity motor cycle can be considered ideal for the same ride-to-work trip but can also double as a machine quite capable of long touring trips. For those with longer daily travel and a definite touring programme, machines in the 175 to 350 cc category fill the bill.

The smallest practical motor cycle for long distance work is the 250 cc size. Although some 125 cc models are now capable of speeds over 100 km/h (62 miles/h) gradients and headwinds will cut this drastically.

Where a pillion passenger is to be carried over long distances an owner should look to a machine of 350 or 500 cc. The more powerful 750, 850 and 1000 cc machines are capable of

*UK gal = 4.5 litres   US gal = 3.7 litres

sustained high speed for hours on end with or without a pillion passenger.

The minimum size of machine best suited for carrying a pillion passenger would be the 250 cc size.

In buying a small-capacity machine should one opt for a two-stroke or a four-stroke?

Without the mighty Honda corporation there would be little choice, for they alone of the big manufacturers offer small-capacity four-strokes.

With the advances made in two-stroke design, the choice should lead towards a two-stroke engine for a small-capacity machine but Honda technology is such that their small four-strokes are equally trouble free, and at least as economical, as their two-stroke counterparts.

Does the same hold true of the medium- and large-capacity machines?

Medium-capacity machines from 125 to 500 cc are produced in two-stroke and four-stroke forms and there is little to choose between them as far as economy and performance is concerned.

In the realm of the big 650 cc and upwards machine, the four-stroke begins to have a decided advantage.

Although there is no reason why large-capacity two-stroke engines should perform any better or worse than their four-stroke competitors, the two-stroke does tend to have a less-favourable fuel consumption and this is one of the principle reasons why the Honda 750 cc, Kawasaki 1000 cc and BMW 900 cc machines tend to outsell the 750 cc Kawasaki and the 750 cc Suzuki two-strokes.

Is there any point in buying a machine capable of more than the legal maximum speed limit allowed in any particular country?

Although the highest speed limit in Britain is currently 113 km/h (70 miles/h) a machine capable of only this speed would be hard put to cope with gradients and, in effect, would only be able to cruise for long periods at something like 16 to 24 km/h (10 to 15 miles/h) below this figure. A good rule is to buy a machine with a maximum speed of some 32 to 40 km/h (20 to 25 miles/h) more than that which one would normally consider using.

This gives a handy reserve of power in the case of an emergency and also means that the machine will not be overtaxing itself during normal running.

What advantage in economy is there in a four-stroke engine?

Generally speaking one can expect a four-stroke to give something like 20 kilometres per litre more. However, overhaul costs tend to be higher due to the greater number of moving parts inside the four-stroke reciprocating-piston engine.

Should one buy a new machine or look for a second-hand one?

This is purely a question of economics. With a new machine there should be no mechanical problems for quite some time. But good second-hand models do exist and if sought out can result in considerable savings.

The current trend of motor-cycle design, whereby new models are produced every year, means that quite a high turnover of quality one-year-old models can be found in many dealers.

What are the most noticeable current trends in motor-cycle design?

Three trends are having a considerable influence on the machines available from the various manufacturers.

Firstly, given the fuel situation, the economy of the small, commuter motor cycle is now an important consideration in the selection of a form of transport. Many owners switched from cars to motor cycles - often using the motor cycle as a second vehicle - during the drastic 1974/75 increase in the price of petrol.

Secondly, the large-capacity touring motor cycle has become something of a status symbol amongst the young and wealthy. This is breeding a new, ultra-sophisticated race of super-bikes, some costing much more than quite exotic motor cars.

Thirdly, although it had its roots in America, there is now a world-wide demand for off-road motor cycles, used either for their original purpose of exploring rough terrain or, and more usually, simply following a fashion of the type enjoyed during the big scooter boom of the late 1950s.

Does Japan now make the majority of the world's motor cycles?

Up until the early 1960s the Midlands of England was the centre of the world's motor-cycle manufacture but this has now diminished greatly and Japan has an enormous lead both in production figures and in the range of machinery.

How have Japanese designers influenced current trends?

Japan, when it moved into the motor-cycle manufacturing business, relied heavily on success in motor-cycle racing to get it's brand names known. This racing heritage is still seen today in the use of road machines which a few years earlier would have been termed exotic motor cycles. Items which a few years ago were the sole prerogative of the racing machine - e.g. overhead camshafts, five- and six-speed gearboxes - are now quite normal in the production machines coming out of Japan.

Are there less exotic machines produced for purely utilitarian use?

Whilst Japan has concentrated on developing machines of high performance, other countries have concentrated on keeping down costs and giving good fuel consumption at the expense of high speed.

Machines from Eastern Europe, such as CZ and Jawa from Czechoslovakia, MZ from East Germany and the range of Russian motor cycles are exceptional value for money, having low initial cost and, because the engines are not highly stressed, low maintenance outlay as well.

How do the Eastern European countries produce low-price machines?

The Russians, East Germans and Czechoslovakians have kept the price of their machines down by concentrating on relatively few designs which have, with only minor detail improvements, remained static for some years.

Whilst the Japanese tend to produce new designs every year with very little or no interchangeability of parts with earlier models the Eastern European machinery obviously needs very little re-tooling from year to year.

To some extent this means that the Eastern European machines are out of date. They rely for their sales on giving exceptional value for money and are doing very well with sales following the increase in the price of fuel.

Is Japanese motor-cycling technology more advanced than that of Europe?

On the evidence of the machines produced this would certainly appear to be the case. Whilst Japan is producing multi-cylinder, overhead-camshaft machines with self starters and other luxury fittings, it was only in 1975 that Britain's sole major manufacturer, Norton-Villiers-Triumph, to some extent, updated their two-and three-cylinder range by fitting electric starters. The same is true of most other European manufacturers who tend to produce detailed improvements rather than completely new machines each year.

How can the Japanese make such big advances?

The Japanese boom was heralded by the introduction of low-cost, super-economical commuter machines.

Tooling up for these was possible because of the vast home-market potential that existed in Japan itself. The companies were guaranteed sufficient sales to cover costs and to make an initial profit. Sales over and above this, which went in exports, enabled them to invest in vast factories, with the most modern of computer tooling.

From there the Japanese industry mushroomed. They became the trend-setters of the world's motor-cycle producers and are currently making sufficient profits to enable them to re-design their ranges over relatively short periods.

What machines are still produced in Britain?

The Norton-Villiers-Triumph combine, set up with government aid in 1974, is the only large-capacity producer of machines in Britain. In 1975 they had two basic models, a 850 cc Norton fitted with electric starter and an 850 cc Triumph also with push-button starting mechanism.

Of the smaller manufacturers only Greaves produced their own engine and only in very limited numbers for off-road competition use.

Are there no mopeds or small-capacity motor cycles produced in Britain?

Since the demise of the BSA Bantam engine and the decision to cease production of the 250 cc Villiers two-stroke, there are no two-stroke engines mass produced in Britain. The last 250 cc motor cycle made in this country was the BSA Triumph single-cylinder four-stroke which has now been discontinued.

Are sidecars still produced?

There are some small manufacturers still producing sidecars but the increase in affluence throughout the world has resulted in the majority of the former sidecar-buying market going over to small cars.

What was the disadvantage of a sidecar?

With the increase in performance of small cars and lower prices which put them within reach of the majority of the public, sidecars ceased to have any real point. With a sidecar the manoeuvrability and traffic-threading facility of a motor cycle disappears to a large extent, and many insurance companies who previously gave up to 50% discount if a sidecar was fitted to a machine, have now reduced these favourable terms considerably.

Can a sidecar be fitted to any machine?

It is generally considered that a 250 cc machine is hard-pressed to carry a sidecar but anything over this capacity can do so. However, many of today's larger machines are built with solo use in mind.

Whereas 20 years ago a designer would build a frame for both solo and sidecar use, today some manufacturers state that their machines are not suitable for sidecar use. In fact, fitting a sidecar invalidates many guarantees.

2
ENGINES

What types of engine are currently in use in motor-cycle and moped manufacture?

There have been diesel and even steam machines produced but today three types of motive-power are used: two-stroke petrol engines, four-stroke petrol engines, and electric power for very small, commuter machines.

Can four-strokes be split into further categories?

There are two categories, the traditional reciprocating-piston, four-stroke engine and the Wankel rotary engine which is a recent invention. In 1975 three manufacturers had these in production and many more were experimenting with prototypes.

How does the reciprocating-piston four-stroke engine work?

The four strokes are induction, compression, combustion and exhaust.

On the first, the induction stroke, the piston descends with the inlet valve open, drawing in the fuel mixture.

For the second, the upward stroke, the valve closes and the mixture is compressed.

As the piston nears the top of its stroke, the vapour is compressed and fired by the sparking plug and the following pressure forces the piston down again for the power, or combustion, stroke.

As the piston rises again the exhaust valve is open allowing the spent gases to pass from the combustion chamber.

How does the Wankel engine differ?

The Wankel engine has a triangular rotor, revolving eccentrically in a specially-shaped housing to form three moving combustion chambers. The rotor is geared to an internal shaft on which it is eccentrically mounted so that the shaft turns three times to each revolution of the rotor.

The revolving of the rotor expands and contracts the space between its face and the chamber twice during each revolution. The first expansion forms the induction phase when fuel mixture is sucked in. The following contraction compresses the charge which is ignited and the resulting pressure provides the motive power and the combustion phase. The cycle is completed by the second contraction phase during which the spent gases are expelled from the chamber.

What are the advantages and disadvantages of the Wankel engine over the traditional four-stroke unit?

Because of its lack of reciprocating parts, the rotary engine is smoother in operation and should, eventually, prove less expensive to produce. It is ideally suited to motor cycle use in that it is more compact and lighter, for a given power output, than a reciprocating-piston engine.

To some extent the Wankel is still in an experimental stage and engines tend to be more complex and expensive than they are likely to be in the near future when more research has been completed. The main problem with the Wankel is in providing a low wear rate seal between the rotor and the chamber.

Can reciprocating-piston four-strokes be further sub-divided?

Such engines are usually categorised by the position and method of operation of the valves.

Side valves have all but disappeared from production as

power output and fuel consumption is inferior to that of overhead valve designs.

Overhead valve engines can be divided into those with push-rod operation of the valves and those with an overhead camshaft mounted in the cylinder-head assembly.

Which of the two valve-operation designs is the most popular?

Once almost the sole prerogative of the racing and super-sports machine, the overhead camshaft is now rapidly taking over from the push-rod engine. With the camshaft mounted in the cylinder head, push rods and sometimes, rocker arms are eliminated, thereby reducing the operating weight of the valve mechanism and allowing increased engine revolutions.

Overhead camshafts also allow lower spring pressures for the valves, reducing power loss and increasing valve-seat life.

Are there any alternatives to valve springs?

Desmodromic systems have been tried whereby the valves are closed mechanically as well as opened mechanically, eliminating the possibility of valve bounce but adding greatly to manufacturing costs.

Are there any disadvantages to overhead-camshaft engines?

Because of the greater amount of machining on the cylinder head, ohc designs tend to be more expensive to produce and are generally more complex. The valve timing needs to be re-set when the cylinder is removed even for something as simple as valve grinding or a de-coke.

How do two-stroke engines differ from four-stroke engines?

While a four-stroke engine delivers a power stroke for every two revolutions of the crankshaft, a two-stroke engine has one power stroke for each revolution.

Can two-stroke engines be sub-divided?

There is no such clear division as with the reciprocating-piston and Wankel four-stroke engines. However, from the point of view of motor cycle use, engines can be split into those having a separate oil-metering system with its own tank for lubricant and those where the oil has to be pre-mixed with petrol and then share a common fuel tank.

What are the advantages of the two-stroke design over the four-stroke engine?

Up until the mid-1950s, the two-stroke engine was generally considered fit only for utilitarian purpose but since that date much development work has been done resulting in units which can surpass, size-for-size, the power outputs of four-stroke engines.

Advances in fuel and oil technology have also helped reliability and longevity of the two-stroke engine, particularly in cutting down the need for decarbonisation of the combustion chamber and exhaust system.

With less moving parts - no valve-gear or valve-train mechanics - the two-stroke engine is less expensive to manufacture.

Has the two-stroke engine any serious disadvantages?

Two big ones. Exhaust emissions from two-stroke engines are considerably greater - as oil is burnt in the fuel - and petrol consumption usually tends to be greater than on a four-stroke machine of the same size.

How does the oil-metering system work?

An oil pump driven from the crankshaft is usually controlled by the throttle, the twist grip having two cables, one to the pump and the other to the carburettor.

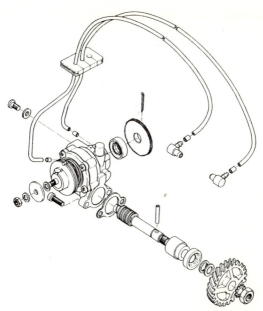

Fig. 1. A complex two-stroke oil pump from Yamaha. More to go wrong and expensive to produce but worthwhile for it meets an engines oil needs at all engine speeds.

What are the advantages and disadvantages of this system?

At low throttle openings only a small amount of oil is metered to the fuel and as engine speed and throttle opening increase, the amount of oil is stepped up. Because oil is matched to engine requirements, such a system uses less lubricant than a petrol-oil-mix machine. The reduction in the amount of oil used also means that there is less tendancy for carbon deposits to build up in the combustion chamber and exhaust ports.

Another asset is that fuel from normal petrol pumps can be used without the need for pre-mixing with oil or using special forecourt dispensers. The possibility of neat oil globules settling in the carburettor or fuel tank is removed.

The only disadvantages are the initial cost and the fact that 'the pump is something else that can go wrong'. In fact, the units are generally very reliable. However, most highly stressed racing engines still rely on pre-mixed fuels.

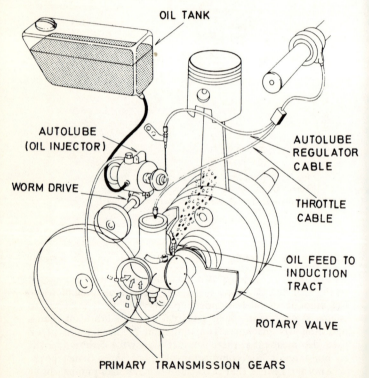

Fig. 2. Diagrammatic layout of a two-stroke automatic oiling system

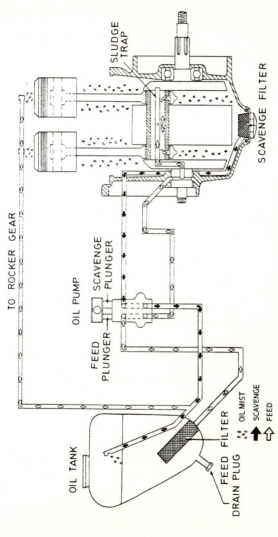

Fig. 3. Typical oiling system of a four stroke. This model uses a plunger pump

How are motor-cycle engines measured?

In early times a formula was used to determine horsepower but, nowadays, the cubic capacity of the engine is the common method of categorisation.

How is the cubic capacity worked out?

This is the volume swept by the piston's upward movement in the cylinder. Therefore the capacity of a machine is the piston's stroke multipled by the cross-section area of the piston, multiplied, in the case of multi-cylinder machines, by the number of cylinders.

Do most motor cycles have only one cylinder?

Until the 1960s the majority of machines were of either single- or twin-cylinder design, but currently three- and four-cylinder machines are being built in greater numbers and are enjoying a vogue.

What are the advantages and disadvantages of three-and four-cylinder engines?

It is obviously more expensive to build multi-cylinder engines and more attention must be paid to finning if the inside cylinders are to run at the same temperature as those on the outside of the engine.
    The great advantage of the three-and four-cylinder engines is that power pulses are smoother and therefore the power unit should suffer less from vibration.

What cylinder layout designs are used in modern engines?

Just about every possible layout is in use by one manufacturer or another. Currently, single-cylinder engines are available with the cylinder upright and horizontal.

How are twin-cylinder engines arranged?

The vertical, parallel-twin engine was pioneered by the British Triumph company in the mid-1930s and their current twins are, in fact, direct descendants of that original 500 cc model.

Not all parallel twins are vertical, however, as many manufacturers, including Norton, and Honda, have inclined the engines forward.

Parallel twins fall easily into two categories - those with crankshafts with in-line crankpins and those with the pins at 180°.

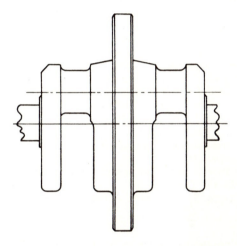

Fig. 4. On most British four-stroke parallel twins, the crankshaft has in-line crankpins

What are the relative merits of each crankpin arrangement?

With in-line crankpins, both pistons travel up and down together with the cylinders firing alternately. This gives evenly-spaced, 360° firing strokes.

Engine balance is improved and vibration reduced with 180° pins but this system results in firing-impulse intervals of 180° and 540°.

Two-stroke engines of parallel-twin design are usually built with 180° crankshafts and, as the engines fire on each downstroke of each piston, provide even, 180° firing intervals.

Are two-cylinder engines produced in other forms?

Other mass-built systems are the vee-twin and flat-twin.

Many vee-twin models were built in the early days of the motor-cycle industry but then the type all but died out. It has been revised in recent years but the Italian Moto Guzzi company with a vee-twin car engine set across the frame and by the Italian Ducati concern who have a vee-twin with the cylinders in line with the chassis.

Twin-cylinder engines with the cylinders opposed have been produced for many years by the German BMW factory and are now being made by the Russian Ural concern.

The Russian machine is virtually a copy of an early BMW layout. The current BMW machine, with its engine set transversely across the frame, is renowned for its smooth running, having near-perfect balance.

Opposed twins have been manufactured with the cylinders in line with the frame, notably by Douglas in the 1920s but there is currently no manufacturer offering this type of machine.

Are there any three-cylinder engines in production?

It is only in recent years that three-cylinder engines have begun to enjoy a vogue.

First in the field with quantity production were BSA and Triumph with a three-cylinder four-stroke engine based on the earlier 500 cc Triumph Twin. This was followed by a 750 cc three-cylinder four-stroke engine from the Italian Laverda factory - also a development from an earlier, smaller, two-cylinder design.

Currently the Japanese Kawasaki and Suzuki companies

are producing three-cylinder two-stroke designs, the Suzuki 750 cc being water cooled.

What are the advantages of the three-cylinder engine?

The main advantage of a three-cylinder engine is that the crankshaft crankpins can be set at 120° throws to give even firing impulses every 120° on two-stroke units and 240° on four-stroke engines, doing away with any irregular running at low engine speeds.

Another advantage, from a design point of view, is that a three-cylinder engine requires very little extra room over a twin-cylinder layout.

What four-cylinder machines are produced?

Although four-cylinder engines once enjoyed a vogue, particularly with the Ariel machine, it is only in recent years that the 'four' has again come into prominence.

Many Japanese manufacturers now offer four-cylinder designs most with transversely-mounted engines.

Honda have also recently introduced a flat-four engine with the cylinders mounted transversely in two banks of two.

Has the four-cylinder engine any advantages?

Very few. A transversely-mounted four-cylinder engine has a large engine width and frontal area and the complexity of such units - particularly in regard to carburation and ignition timing - put fine tuning out of the range of the private owner who usually has his machine serviced by specialists with expensive electronic-diagnostic equipment.

Is there any advance on four-cylinders?

There have been six-and eight-cylinder racing engines produced by Honda and Moto Guzzi respectively, but the largest number of cylinders offered on a road machine is the six used to power the latest 750 cc Benelli.

Again the engine is mounted across the frame and judging by the delay between its first announcement and its still-to-come quantity production the factory is running into considerable difficulties with the design.

Are electric mopeds practical?

Ecologically, electric vehicles are a blessing, creating no pollution hazards and not necessarily dependent on natural resources for their fuel.

However, electric machines are unlikely to be used in greater numbers until scientists can produce lighter batteries with better power capacity. This is because electric machines are limited to about 50 kilometre trips with re-charging between journeys.

The power consumption of these machines increases dramatically as speed increases. Thus, the machines have not yet been developed sufficiently for any form of touring or even lengthy commuting.

Is water cooling used on motor cycles?

Yes, but is only offered on very few machines because of the extra complications and cost of adding a water jacket, radiator, hoses and pump.

Does water cooling have any great advantages?

Because of a motor cycle's basic design, the engine is very much in the air stream and adequately cooled. However, water cooling is advantageous in keeping down running temperatures, particularly on multi-cylinder two-stroke engines. It is also a great noise insulator and was used on the LE Velocette two-cylinder machine which was renowned for its silent running.

3
CARBURATION

What types of carburettor are used on motor cycles?

The two most commonly used carburettors are the normal slide-operated-throttle type and the vacuum carburettor where the air slide is operated by the suction from the inlet tract.

Has fuel injection been used on motor-cycle engines?

There are no production machines featuring fuel injection but certain proprietory instruments of a fuel-injector type have been marketed by accessory manufacturers.

Are there any advantages in fuel injectors?

Considerable advantages are claimed but it is often found that whilst it is possible to set a 'fuel injector' to give greater economy or greater performance, it is not always possible to combine the two virtues.

It is also true that it is possible to do the same with a normal carburettor.

What is the most common carburettor in use on British machines?

For many years British machines have almost exclusively used carburettors made by the Amal company. The most recent of these, the Concentric series, is employed on the three-cylinder

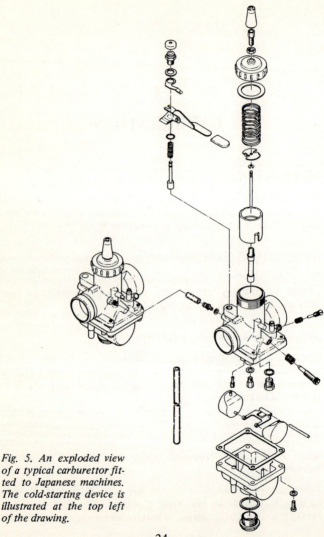

Fig. 5. An exploded view of a typical carburettor fitted to Japanese machines. The cold-starting device is illustrated at the top left of the drawing.

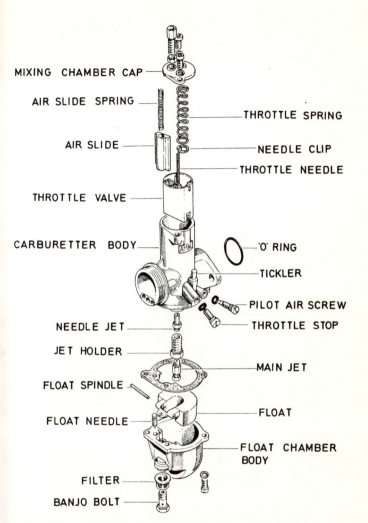

Fig. 6. Latest in the long line of Amal carburettors. This is the Concentric version as fitted to all current British machines

Triumphs and the two-cylinder Norton machines from the Norton-Villiers-Triumph combine.

The Amal Monobloc was introduced in 1955 and became virtually a standard fitment on British four-stroke machines until 1967.

As the name suggests, the Monobloc is a unit-construction carburettor having the float chamber integral with the mixing chamber.

Both the Monobloc and Concentric carburettors are through-the-valve types.

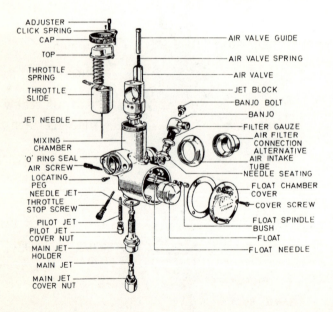

Fig. 7. The Amal Monobloc which preceded the current Concentric series

What is the advantage of the integral carburettor?

Carburettors with separate float chambers, often mounted some small distance from the carburettor, tend to suffer from a rise and fall in float level at the main jet when the machine is canted over. The Monobloc with its integral float chamber all but obviated this.

What are the advantages of the Concentric carburettor?

The Concentric carburettor goes a stage further than the Monobloc in having its float chamber directly underneath the main jet and throttle needle. Therefore, even greater degrees of lean are possible with the machine before the level in the float chamber at the jet point is affected.

What are the adjustments on Amal carburettors?

Two infinitely variable adjustments are provided, one for the idling speed and the other for adjusting the mixture at idling revolutions.

How can one differentiate between these two adjusting screws?

On Amal Monobloc and Concentric carburettors the throttle-stop screw for adjusting the idling speed is inclined upwards. On Monobloc carburettors the screw setting is maintained by a sleeve spring over the screw shank. On the Concentric series the head of the screw is held by friction created by a nylon ring within the carburettor body.

How are the adjustments made?

To increase the idling speed, the throttle screw is turned clockwise into the carburettor. Unscrewing the screw, counterclockwise, reduces the idling speed by allowing the throttle slide to sit lower in the carburettor tract.

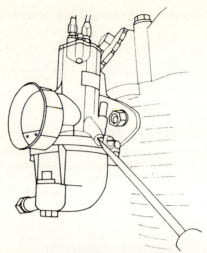

Fig. 8. Throttle-slide stop adjustment on the Amal Concentric. The adjusting screw immediately to the right of the screwdriver point is for the slow-running air/petrol mixture

The idling-mixture adjustment provides for richer and leaner mixtures at tickover speeds. The screw should be turned clockwise, inwards, to richen the mixture.

What is the setting for the idling screw?

The best way to adjust the idling mixture is to start the machine, turn the mixture screw fully clockwise into the carburettor and then unscrew, with the engine at tickover, until the exhaust beat hesitates. If the screw is now turned inwards by three-quarters of a turn the setting will be correct.

Are there other adjustments on Amal carburettors?

The throttle-stop screw and mixture screw together with the throttle needle are the only items which can be adjusted. On

Amal Concentric carburettors the needle has three positions whilst on the earlier Monobloc it has five.

Fig. 9. Needle adjustment on a Concentric carburettor is by three notches for the locating clip—the higher the needle, the richer the mixture

Other settings may be made by changing the throttle slide and the main jet but these necessitate replacement of parts.

How do the various adjustments affect the carburation at different throttle openings?

The first one-eighth of the throttle response is governed by the idling air screw. From one-eighth to one-quarter, the throttle cutaway is responsible, the smaller the cutaway the richer the mixture. The throttle response from one-quarter to

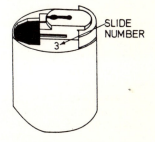

Fig. 10. The cutaway on an Amal slide is indicated at the top of the slide itself

three-quarters open is dependent upon the position of the needle, the lower the needle the weaker the mixture. The final three-quarters to fully-open response is governed by the size of the main jet.

How is it possible to ascertain the correct size of the main jet?

For most practical purposes the size quoted by the manufacturer of the machine will be accurate. However, where machines are used in excessively hot or cold climates or where a special has been built using a non-standard carburettor, a test for main-jet size may be made as follows. The machine should be driven in an intermediate gear at full throttle and then the throttle quickly closed and the engine cut. The condition of the sparking plug will then give a clue as to any modification necessary to the main jet.

A very sooty black plug will indicate that too much fuel is reaching the engine and that a smaller size jet will not only pay dividends in terms of performance, but also in economy. A white, flakey-deposited plug indicates the opposite - that the machine is being starved of fuel at high revs, a dangerous state for it indicates that the engine is running too weakly and is therefore overheating.

Carburettor main jets may be increased or decreased until the ideal dark-brown deposit is indicated on the plug check. As a safety measure the main jet should then be increased by between 5 and 10 per cent over the ideal as an aid to cool running.

How often should the carburettor be cleaned?

The amount of sediment and foreign matter that collects in a carburettor depends primarily on the effectiveness of the filter or filters between the fuel tank and the carburettor float bowl. Some machines have fuel tank filters and also an auxiliary filter in the carburettor itself. These will require less cleaning than those with one filter only. The condition of the inside of the fuel tank will also affect cleaning intervals. A tank which has interior rust - not an uncommon thing - will lead to large quantities of sediment appearing in the carburettor.

A check should be made, initially every 800 km, until it is seen just how much sediment is reaching the float chamber.

Fig. 11. When replacement of the Concentric float bowl is made with the carburettor still on the machine, care must be taken to ensure that the gasket is in position and that the float pivot-shaft is correctly located in its grooves in the bowl

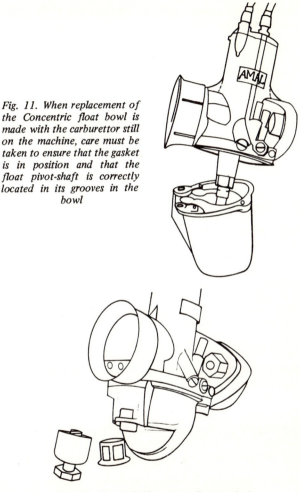

Fig. 12. The fuel filter on a Concentric is housed in the banjo union where the fuel line meets the float chamber

What are the advantages of one carburettor per cylinder on multi-cylinder machines?

The main advantage is in the free flow of vapour from the carburettor, past the inlet valve, to the combustion chamber. Where one carburettor is used on a twin-cylinder machine the inlet tract has to be bifurcated and this can lead to turbulance in the tract which restricts the amount of fuel flowing to the cylinder.

Also, even on a well-built engine, it is possible that one cylinder will demand a different carburettor setting than its neighbour. With multi-carburettors it is possible to set each instrument precisely to the demands of the cylinder it serves.

Are there any disadvantages in multi-carburettors?

Obviously one instrument per cylinder is more costly than a shared carburettor. As the number of cylinders on engines increases and the number of carburettors goes up, the problem of tuning becomes more and more difficult. In fact, on some of the four-cylinder Japanese designs, carburettor tuning, is perhaps, better left to the particular company's specialists who will have a selection of special vacuum instruments designed to aid such tuning.

Can carburettors be synchronised without the aid of sophisticated equipment?

With two carburettors on a twin-cylinder machine there is not a great problem but when the number of carburettors reaches three or four the problem becomes more acute.

What is the procedure for synchronising twin carburettors?

Slacken off the throttle-stop screws so that both slides can fully close. To ensure that there is no pressure on the slide the carburettor cable to the twist grip should be adjusted so that there is backlash in the assembly.

Next, one sparking plug lead should be removed, the engine started on the other cylinder and its carburettor adjusted for idling speed and mixture. If a revolution counter is fitted to the machine, attempt to regulate the engine at its lowest, non-hesitating speed.

Repeat the procedure with the other cylinder. Now the machine should be started on both cylinders and, if the idling speed is too great, both throttle-stop screws should be released, counter-clockwise, by an equal amount. Take up the slack on each carburettor cable at its adjuster in turn until there is a just-perceptible increase in engine revs. Each adjuster should then be backed off one complete turn.

Theoretically, both throttle slides should now begin to operate at the same time. To check this, place a finger on each slide and ask a colleague to slowly open the throttle. If both slides do not commence to move at the same time the back-lash in the carburettor cable of the late operating slide should be reduced until both slides are synchronised.

Is there any method for avoiding the results of slide out of synchronisation at idling speeds?

Norton, BSA and Triumph twins have been fitted for some years with a balance tube between the inlet manifolds. This, in effect, acts as a compensator, and synchronisation of carburettors at idling speeds is not so critical.

Is there an easy and safe way to increase fuel economy?

The quickest, and a relatively safe, method of increasing fuel economy at the cost of a slight loss in engine response is to lower the carburettor needle by one notch.

Do carburettors on foreign machines follow the same principles?

The majority of Japanese carburettors are of similar type but

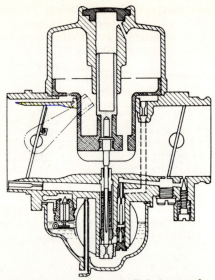

Fig. 13. A vacuum-controlled piston carburettor as used on some Japanese machines. This model was employed on the CB450 Honda

on certain Honda models, for example, a vacuum-controlled piston with butterfly throttle valve is used.

On Japanese manual-slide carburettors, are the running adjustments the same as with British Amal instruments?

The basic throttle-stop and idling-mixture adjustments are similar but often, on Japanese machines, the throttle-stop screw is situated at the top of the mixing chamber.

How does the vacuum-controlled piston carburettor function?

The throttle cable is connected to a butterfly valve which, when opened, allows the vacuum created by the descending piston to raise the carburettor slide against the pressure of its spring.

Connected to the slide is a needle which limits the flow of fuel from the float chamber.

How are adjustments made on these carburettors?

Vacuum-controlled piston carburettors have an idling screw for tickover adjustment. Turning this screw inwards, clockwise, weakens the mixture. The screw should be adjusted for the fastest idle speed and this then slowed to the best tickover rate by means of the stop screw on the butterfly.

How are the various parts of the vacuum-controlled piston carburettor related to engine speed?

The idling mixture screw affects engine speed at low throttle openings. The position of the throttle needle - normally adjustable in one of three or five grooves - decides throttle response from medium- to high-speed range. At maximum speed the throttle response is governed by the size of the main jet.

Are any other types of carburettor currently in use on motor cycles?

The only British machines to have been fitted, in recent•times, with a non-Amal carburettor were the Villiers engines used in certain Francis-Barnett, James, Excelsior and other medium-capacity machines and the Triumph motor cycles which from 1952 to 1958 used an SU carburettor on their 650 cc Thunderbird machines. The SU was a vacuum-controlled piston instrument, similar in principle to those used on certain Japanese machines today but with adjustments made as follows.

The idling speed is adjusted by a spring-loaded stop screw and the idling mixture weakened by turning the jet lever stop nut at the base of the mixing chamber upwards, clockwise.

Do these carburettors need special maintenance?

A few drops of light oil or Redex should be added to the chamber at the top of the piston every 3000 km.

How often should carburettors need adjusting?

Apart from dramatic changes in climatic conditions, carburettors should, theoretically, not need adjustment. This however, does not take into account wear within the carburettor itself, the ingress of sediment from the fuel tank which will affect performance, wear and tear on other parts of the engine which can be counteracted by re-adjustment of the air/fuel mixture.

What are the most likely carburation faults?

Most suspected carburation faults are found to be the result of malfunctions in other parts of the machine. Badly-set or pitted contact-breaker points can often give symptoms similar to those of poor carburation. Before any attempt is made to adjust a carburettor the ignition system should always be investigated.

Poor idling performance which cannot be corrected by use of the throttle-stop screw or the idling-mixture adjustment is often the fault of a slight air leak at the carburettor manifold.

On Amal Monobloc instruments over-tightening of the flange nuts could lead to bowing of the carburettor flange face, thus producing an air leak.

Can such a bowed flange be repaired?

Do not attempt to file the face but simply lay a sheet of emery cloth or wet-and-dry paper on a flat surface - a piece of plate glass is ideal - and carefully rub the carburettor flange face across it in a circular motion until it is seen that the whole of the face has been in contact with the abrasive. When replacing the carburettor, remember that the flange is now thinner than it was previously and will be more likely to bow if excessive tightening takes place.

The Amal Monobloc and Concentric carburettors rely on a rubber 'O' ring mounted in a recess in the flange face for an

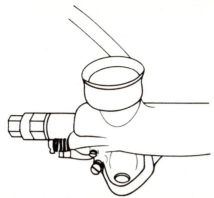

Fig. 14. A bowed flange on a carburettor can be made good by gently rubbing the face on a flat surface covered with an abrasive compound

air-tight seal. This, in effect, means that excessive tightening is unnecessary. As long as good quality locking nuts are used, it is only necessary to nip them up gently.

What is the most likely cause of sticking carburettors?

Lack of care when assembling the throttle slide can result in burrs or a deformed slide which may then stick in the carburettor body. If this is the case, there is very little chance of repairing such damage - apart from the filing down of small burrs - and a replacement slide should be fitted.

On many twin-carburettor set-ups, the ideal strength of the throttle-slide return springs have been reduced to give an easier throttle movement at the handlebar. Often when a little wear takes place this spring pressure becomes insufficient and the replacing of the weak springs with a heavier variety can often effect a cure.

Poor cable routeing from the handlebar twist-grip to the carburettor itself can often result in a sticking throttle. Make sure that the route of the cable has no sharp bends or kinks, particularly where the cable enters the tank tunnel at the headstock.

On excessively worn carburettors, throttle sticking may become evident as a result of the slide holding itself in the jet block by the sheer vibration of the engine.

4
IGNITION SYSTEMS

What is the purpose of the ignition system?

The ignition system is designed to provide a spark which ignites the petrol/air vapour in the combustion chamber. Not only is it necessary for the spark to be of the correct intensity, it must always occur at the right time.

What sort of ignition systems are used in motor cycles?

Once the most popular form of ignition, the magneto, has all but disappeared from current production. It was used on most large-capacity British machines until the mid-1960s. Other systems include coil ignition, energy transfer, capacitor discharge, and transistor systems.

Why has the magneto now disappeared?

Although the magneto was an efficient instrument, it was bulky, difficult to drive, and expensive to manufacture.

How was the spark advanced at high revs on a magneto?

Two systems were employed, manual, and automatic.
   The manual system of advance was effected by means of a cable and handlebar lever. The automatic system relied on bobweights throwing out when the revs reached a certain point and advancing the contact-breaker cam.

What system replaced the magneto?

An attempt was made to experiment with a system known as energy transfer.

What were its advantages?

One of the advantages of the energy-transfer set-up was that, like the magneto, it provides a spark of increasing energy as the revs of the engine rose and the machine ignition demands increased.

The energy-transfer system as used on competition Triumphs developed for the Internation Six Days Trial was easily mounted with the coils bolted to the crankcase and a rotor revolving within them, driven by the crankshaft itself.

What were the disadvantages of this system?

With the coils mounted on the crankcase, they were prone to suffer from vibration and although this was cured by encapsulating them, the system, to work at its best and to give easy starting, demanded an ignition timing far more ciritical then a magneto or any other system.

What are the forms of ignition system used today?

The coil-ignition system, as used on most cars, is the most popular method of providing the spark in current design.

What are the advantages of this system?

The main advantages of a coil-ignition set-up is that it provides a good spark at low engine-cranking speeds, and therefore is a boon in starting. The system is virtually trouble free and does not require the critical ignition timing of the energy-transfer set-up.

Has coil ignition any disadvantages?

Although some machines are fitted with a form of emergency

starting, a flat battery will often mean that a coil-ignition-equipped machine cannot be kick started. It is therefore imperative on coil-ignition machines to ensure that the battery is kept fully charged.

The only other disadvantage of the traditional coil ignition is that it continues to rely on a contact breaker which is prone to wear and demands regular cleaning and adjustment.

Is there any ignition system which does away with a contact breaker?

The current trend is towards a form of contact-breaker-less ignition where a transistorised electronic circuit triggers the spark.

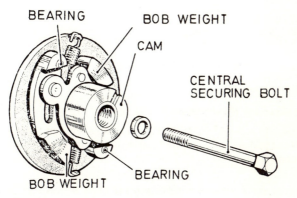

Fig. 15. A simple centrifugal ignition advance unit from Lucas

Can any form of ignition advance be built into such systems?

Again transistors come into play and can provide a continuously variable ignition advance - from the moment the engine is started to its peak rev limits.

Is there no way in which a coil-ignition system can be modified to provide starting current with a flat battery?

Lucas in England have developed a capacitor system for their 12 V systems which gives an adequate spark for starting.

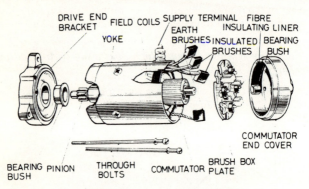

Fig. 16. British-made Lucas starter motor

Are there any disadvantages to this system?

It involves a considerable number of components and therefore cost is a factor. Installation of the various parts on the machine can also be a problem.

What systems are used to distribute the spark on multi-cylinder designs?

There are two systems, one being a common, car-type distributor with an internal rotor. This was in use principally on the Triumph machines of the early 1960s.

The most usual method of providing spark distribution for multi-cylinder engines today is to provide more than one contact-breaker assembly. Two or more contact-breaker assemblies are usually mounted on the same back plate and share a common opening cam.

Are there any disadvantages to this system?

A large number of points assemblies is obviously costly and miniaturisation of the parts makes maintenance difficult.

Clearly the future of motor-cycle ignition systems lies in the field of the contact-breaker-less system with its transistorised circuitry which can also provide infinitely variable spark advance.

Are there any other advantages to transistorised ignition?

Because there are no points to erode, the transistorised ignition set-up will maintain its ignition timing indefinitely whereas, as the points gap varies on a conventional set-up, the ignition timing is also affected.

Is ignition timing more difficult to set on electronic systems?

To time machines fitted with electronic ignition systems a strobe light is necessary to ensure that the spark is occuring at exactly the right moment.

Such a light can also be used to good advantage on machines fitted with coil ignition. Many manufacturers now mark a rotating component, such as the crankshaft rotor, specifically for strobe use.

What methods are used in motor-cycle design to enable the engine to be started?

Three systems have been used, hand cranking, kick starting and the push-button electrical starter. The hand starter, used on various models of the water-cooled LE Velocette machine is now the sole province of the American Rokon motor cycle on which a rope wound around a pully is used to start the machine up. This was not done for any specific purpose but simply indicates the engine's original concept, that of a stationary unit.

The majority of today's motor cycles are either started by a kick starter or an electric starter.

What are the pros and cons of a kick starter?

Kick starters, being purely mechanical and having had much development work done on them are very reliable and, can start a machine even when its battery is in a low state of charge. However, particularly on larger-capacity machines, a certain degree of effort is necessary to spin the engine and the ever-increasing number of women riders find the electric starters a boon.

What are the pros and cons of the electric starter?

Electric starters pioneered by the Japanese Honda company, are efficient devices which do not put too much of a drain

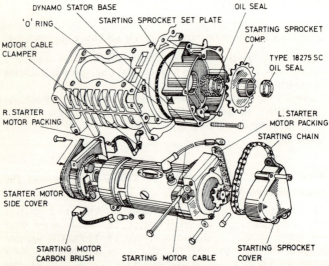

Fig. 17. A Japanese starter motor – this is one of the many versions fitted by Honda

on the battery. However, some attempts to adapt existing kick-starting models to electric starting have not been so successful.

The majority of machines fitted with electric starters also have facility for kick starting. It is often suggested that the engine should be turned over once or twice on the kick starter to ease the load before the electric starter is employed.

Are any particular types of motor cycle more suited than others to electric starting?

A good general rule is that the smaller the cylinders, the more successful electric starting is likely to be.

Are any large-capacity machines fitted with electric starters?

The large multi-cylinder Japanese Suzuki, Honda, Kawasaki and Yamaha models all have electric starters but the number of cylinders, particularly in the four-cylinder machines makes electric starting a much more feasible proposition.

However, some twin-cylinder designs also have electric starting, particularly the BMW, the Moto Guzzi from Italy and the Norton Twin from Britain. These are all twin-cyclinder machines and whilst the electric-starting systems have been designed to operate efficiently they do not spin the engine as well as on a four-cylinder design.

Will the time come when kick starters become completely redundant?

Already two manufacturers do not fit kick starters to their machines. BMW on their big twins have recently dispensed with a kick starter following a re-design of other components, and the vee-twin, across-the-frame engines, used by Moto Guzzi, have never had any kick starting provision. The Moto Guzzi engine was originally designed for a car unit and no allowance was made for the fitting of a kick starter.

In racing most competitors start their machine by running alongside. How does this work?

Racing machines are built to the absolute minimum weight

which means that kick starters and electric starters are not employed. The riders engage a low gear, pull in the clutch and run along pushing the machine until it is moving quickly enough for the engine to spin freely when the clutch is dropped.

Can a road machine be started this way?

This is a reasonable method of starting a machine with a low battery in an emergency but the art of climbing aboard a machine once the engine has fired is not easily attained. For the machine which is reluctant to start, it is far better to find a slope which you can run the machine down as you sit astride it.

5

GEARBOXES

How many gears are used in motor-cycle gearboxes?

The number of gears necessary depends upon the power characteristics of the engine. An engine which develops useable power over a wide range of its revs needs fewer gears than one which has a very narrow power band. Generally speaking, two-stroke engines have narrower power bands than their four-stroke counterparts and require more gears so that the engine can be kept within the power range at all speeds.

Also, the larger the engine the wider its power band is likely to be.

Single-cylinder engines tend to produce more torque and therefore have a wider power band than do multi-cylinder engines and for a given cc, it is likely that a multi-cylinder engine can benefit more from a larger number of ratios.

During the 1950s the motor cycle field was dominated by three- and four-speed gearboxes. But as design progressed and rev limits were pressed higher, power bands became narrower so that it became necessary to increase the number of ratios within the gearbox.

Today, most sports machines boast at least five ratios and the smaller, busier two-stroke machines often have six as standard equipment.

By the use of auxiliary gearboxes, some competition machines have been built with as many as 10 ratios.

Are gearboxes designed as an integral part of the engine?

The so-called unit-construction engine has a gearbox manufactured integrally with the engine. Of today's manufacturers, only Norton cling to the outdated, separate gearbox design.

What are the disadvantages of a separate gearbox?

The separate box normally has to be moved on a pivot to adjust primary chain tension. Because of this, oil sealing

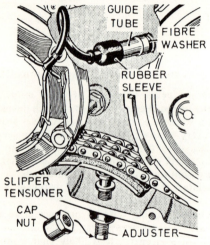

Fig. 18. Most chain-type primary drives now rely on a rubber-faced slipper for tension adjustment

between the gearbox and primary transmission case becomes a problem.

How is chain adjustment effected on a unit-construction gearbox machine?

Some gearboxes, of course, are driven by gears from the engine crankshaft but those with chain drive either have no provision for adjustment or use an adjustable tensioner, usually a steel blade faced with hard rubber which is used to take up slack on the bottom run of the chain.

Do unit-construction designs differ?

The majority of British machines have had their crankcases split vertically but with a separate gearbox chamber which is an integral part of one of the crankcase castings.

What is the advantage of this system?

The main advantage is that the gearbox or the engine can be serviced without the need to dismantle the other components.

Do the Japanese employ the same system?

Japanese engines tend to follow car practice in having a horizontally-split crankcase.

What type of gearbox is used on modern machines?

All modern gearboxes are of the constant-mesh type where the gears are in continual mesh, and gear changes are effected by the engagement of sliding dogs.

What is the advantage of this system?

The gear's teeth in a constant-mesh gearbox are far less likely to suffer damage than in one in which the gear teeth are slid in and out of mesh.

What is meant by wide-, standard- and close-ratio gearboxes?

The terms wide, standard, and close refer to the gaps between the ratios.

A standard set of gearbox ratios would be one for use on the road giving a low enough gear for easy take-off, a high enough top gear to enable reasonable cruising speeds to be attained without unduly stressing the engine, and the intermediate ratios spaced fairly evenly between.

For road racing a low bottom gear is unnecessary as the riders only start from a standstill at the commencement of the event. A lower top gear is desirable so that the engine can produce its peak power at high speed. As the bottom gear is higher and the top gear is lower it is possible to have smaller gaps between the intermediate ratios, allowing the engine to be kept in its power band although, on racing machines, this tends to be considerably narrower than on road machines.

Wide-ratio gearboxes are employed, particularly in the sport of trials, where a rider has to face a number of varying hazards. He will need a choice of three fairly low ratios to enable him to pick the ideal one for climbing a hill, fording a stream, negotiating tight turns or ploughing through mud. The machine also needs a high gear to enable it to be driven on the road without unduly stressing the engine. Because of this the gap between third and fourth, and fourth and fifth gears will be considerably higher than on road and racing machines.

Is foot gear changing now universal?

Yes. All machines currently produced have foot-change gear mechanisms, and all have a positive stop mechanism which returns the lever to the central position after the gear has been engaged.

Are gear levers always placed in identical positions?

Until 1975 manufacturers tended to opt for a gear-lever position of their own liking.

Traditionally, British machines had right-foot gear pedals but when the Japanese began their takeover of the motor-cycle industry, they transferred the gear change to the left-hand side, arguing that as more delicacy was necessary for control of the rear brake it was most likely to be achieved on the right side as the majority of the riders would be right-handed and therefore right-footed.

Why are British manufacturers now changing the gear levers to the left-hand side?

Recent safety-conscious legislation in America has laid down that it is a danger hazard for a rider to change from a machine with the gear lever on one side to a machine with the alternative fitting. It has therefore been laid down that all machines imported into America must, in future, have left-hand gear pedals. As a large percentage of the machines made in Britain are exported to America, British manufacturers are falling in line.

Do all gear levers work in the same direction for raising or lowering the gearing?

Again American legislation is forcing standardisation of this aspect of motor-cycle design but before this incentive to standardisation even British factories with financial links, such as BSA and Triumph, could not agree on a standard form of gear change. BSA traditionally had levers which moved up to lower the ratio and down to raise it. Triumph worked on the converse principle.

Currently, the vast majority of machines are made with an up-for-up and down-for-down gear assembly.

What types of clutches are used on motor cycles?

The most common form of clutch used on modern motor cycles is a multi-plate device running on the gearbox mainshaft.

What is the advantage of this system?

As the clutch is mounted on the mainshaft it is possible for the unit to run at lower than engine speed - up to one-half usually. This allows easier high-speed gear changing, but heavier spring pressure and a larger friction area is necessary than in the case of a clutch mounted on the engine mainshaft as in the majority of car designs.

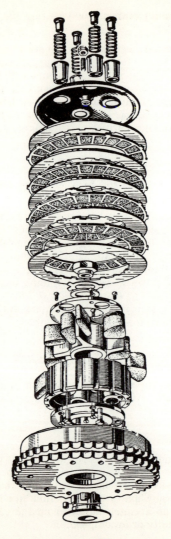

Fig. 19. This typical, multi-plate clutch has a rubber shock absorber built into its centre

Which machines use the car-type clutch?

This clutch is ideally suited to engines in which the crankshaft runs in line with the frame such as in the BMW twins, and the Moto Guzzi.

What type of springs are used in motor-cycle clutches?

The majority of clutches, particularly those of the multi-plate gearbox-mainshaft variety use a number of coil springs - anything from three to six with screwed adjusters, for variation in pressure on the clutch plate.

Is there an alternative to the coil springs?

A diaphragm pressure spring, now found on many car clutches, is currently in use on Norton Twin and Triumph three-cylinder machines.

What are the advantages of the diaphragm spring?

The diaphragm spring system allows for automatic equalisation of the spring pressure across the clutch, requiring no adjustments. It also provides a heavier pressure on the plates with less effort needed to disengage it via the handlebar control lever.

What type of friction materials are used in modern clutches?

Earlier cork and fabric friction material has given way to a composition lining in which asbestos still plays a large part.

How are these linings attached to the clutch plates?

The system of inserting sections of lining into holes machined in the clutch-friction plates has now been discontinued. Sections of friction material are now either bonded to the plates or complete plates built of the composition.

Are there any forms of automatic gearboxes or clutches used on motor cycles?

Automatic centrifugal clutches, where engine speed causes bob weights to throw out and thereby progressively engage the clutch, are common on some small Japanese machines.

Another form of automatic drive, which is being used on some small scooters and mopeds is a centrifugally-operated belt-drive system with expanding and contracting pulleys giving not only an automatic clutch but a stepless variation in gear ratios.

What systems are used to transmit the power from the gearbox to the rear wheel?

There are two basic methods in operation, shaft drive and chain drive.

What are the pros and cons of the shaft and chain drive?

The shaft is considerably more expensive to produce and to replace if damaged in use.

However, it is considerably cleaner than a chain, which

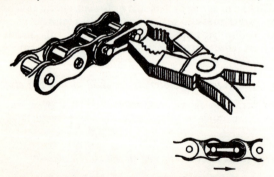

Fig. 20. Pliers are the best tool for removing and fitting chain spring links. When fitted, such a link should always have its closed end facing the normal direction of rotation

must be kept lubricated if its efficiency and life are not to be impaired, and it does not need the frequent adjustment that is necessary with the chain drive.

A chain can pick up road dirt which, with the lubricant on the chain, forms a highly-effective grinding paste. Therefore the need to regularly clean chains is paramount if their life expectancy is to be realised.

With the rapidly-increasing power of modern machines, chains are becoming heavier and considerably more expensive, thereby negating some of the system's advantage over that of the shaft.

Which models feature shaft drive?

Shaft drive has been a hallmark of the German BMW concern for many years. It is also used in the Italian Guzzi vee-twin and in Honda's latest and most exotic four-cylinder model.

6
MOTOR CYCLE PARTS

BRAKES

What types of brakes are used on modern motor cycles?

Up to a short time ago, braking on the vast majority of machines was by means of conventional internal-expanding shoe-and-drum systems.

Was this efficient?

Bearing in mind the performance expectations of the machines up until the last decade, the expanding-shoe assembly was satisfactory but as speeds began to rise manufacturers sought ways of improving brake efficiency.

What was their first solution?

Designers applied themselves principally to the front brake which provides the prime stopping force on any wheeled vehicle: when braking occurs a vast percentage of total weight is transferred to the forward wheels.

The conventional single-lever brake provides one leading shoe and one trailing shoe. The leading shoe has the benefit of an automatic servo action brought about by the rotation of the drum against the stationary shoe.

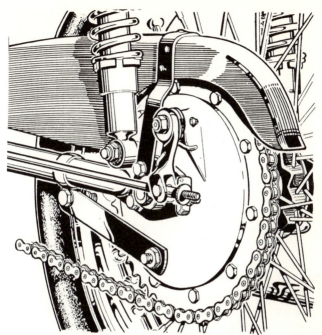

Fig. 21. A typical single-leading-shoe rear brake, with only one cam operated by the pedal

Designers switched to a two-leading-shoe operation with separate cams, linked via the brake cable, for each shoe.

Were there disadvantages to this system?

The main advantage was that it provided an easy updating of existing wheels. Brake plates with two-leading-shoe assemblies could be fitted to existing wheels.

However, the system, whilst providing a considerable advance in braking power, did not get away from the main disadvantage of the drum brake, the build up of heat during operation.

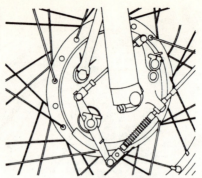

Fig. 22. On a two-leading-shoe brake, the two cams are linked for simultaneous operation

The designers therefore turned their attention to the disc brake, already making its mark in racing-and sports-car use.

What are the advantages of a disc brake?

A disc brake does not have the overheating problems of the drum brake as the friction surfaces where heat is built up are in the air stream.

Another considerable advantage of the disc brake is that its design enables a check to be kept on wear without the need to dismantle the wheel.

Are motor-cycle brakes mechanically or hydraulically operated?

The majority of front disc brakes are operated by a hydraulic line with a fluid reservoir integral with the blade-bar lever.

The majority of rear brakes are operated either by rod or cable from the foot pedal.

What are the advantages of hydraulic operation?

The principle advantage is in eliminating the friction inherent in a cable design.

WHEELS

Are all motor-cycle wheels of the spoke design?

Most wheels are built using either 36 or 40 spokes.

What is the advantage of the spoke wheel?

It offers little wind resistance and is easily repairable, either by truing up or by fitting a new rim, in the event of an accident.

Are any other types of wheels in use?

Recent advances in metallurgy and casting methods have allowed wheels to be made from magnesium castings with integral spoking.

What are the advantages of these magnesium wheels?

At the moment the wheels are extremely costly, being built in very small numbers for competition use for which they are favoured because of their light weight.

If the wheels succeed and are adopted by manufacturers they could then be built in larger quantities and at a price competitive to the normal spoked variety. An added advantage of the one-piece magnesium wheel is that tubeless types could be used, again effecting a saving on initial production cost.

Can spoked wheels be trued by the home mechanic?

The building of spoked wheels is a fine art and not to be undertaken lightly. However, slight truing adjustment of the spoke nipples is quite possible.

The main problem for someone attempting to true a wheel for the first time is to get the rim to run centrally around the hub and in a reasonable vertical plane. The combination of these two virtues can best be achieved by a professional wheel builder.

What types of spokes are used?

Motor-cycle spokes can be divided into two basic types, butted and non-butted.

Butted spokes are those which have an increase in diameter at the point where the spoke is attached to the hub. This is done to increase the strength of the spokes for it is at the hub that most spoke failures occur.

Both classes of spoke can be further sub-divided into straight pull and those where the spoke head is turned at an angle for attachment to the hub.

Straight pull spokes are considerably stronger but lead to manufacturing difficulties in the design of the hub, and are nowadays used on very few machines.

Do spoke failures not occur at the threaded end where the nipple is attached?

Threads on spokes are not cut with a die as are threads on the majority of bolts. To avoid setting up possible fracture points, spoke threads are rolled.

TYRES

How critical are the types and sizes of tyres fitted to motor cycles?

Development during road racing has been responsible for many of the tremendous advances made in tyre design during the past decade. Considerable research has also been made into ideal sizes and profiles of tyres for particular machines, and manufacturer's recommendations should always be followed in these matters. Machines are designed with an optimum tyre size, and alteration to this can result in changing the handling characteristics.

Is tyre wear a critical factor?

The power produced and the acceleration possible with

present-day machines has put a premium on tyre design. Although research engineers have developed tyres, tyre profiles and rubber compounds which give a degree of grip unheard of years ago, tyre wear is still a serious problem. As the amount of rubber-to-road contact with a two-wheeler, which has to be banked for cornering, is limited, the wear is confined to a fairly small section of the tyre.

How important are tyre pressures?

Again much research has been done by machine manufacturers and by tyre engineers into the best pressures for road and racing machines and these should always be adhered to. Tyre pressures are a result of considerable liaison between the machine and the tyre manufacturers and are designed to give the best grip on the road surface and good wearing qualities.

SUSPENSION

What is the purpose of suspension?

A form of suspension to isolate the main body of the motor cycle from road shock transmitted to the wheels has two primary purposes.

It is designed to increase comfort for the rider in preventing road irregularities being transmitted through the machine to his person, and perhaps, more importantly, it is designed to enable the wheels to stay in contact with the road, allowing the machine to ride up and down irregularities rather than flying into the air each time a bump is met.

Do all motor cycles and mopeds have front and rear suspension?

The vast majority of motor cycles have operating suspension at the front and rear although with the more utilitarian mopeds front suspension only is offered by some companies. There is at the time of writing one manufacturer still offering an ultra-utility machine with no form of suspension on either wheel.

What is the normal form of suspension?

The majority of manufacturers feature a form of front springing

Fig. 23. An exploded view of a Girling suspension unit showing the spring assembly on the left and the damper mechanism on the right

with a telescopic fork inside which are springs and a damping mechanism.

What is the purpose of the damping mechanism?

The hydraulic fluid, normally a light-grade oil with anti-frothing additive, is used to prevent excess movement and to dampen out the action of the springs.

Have all telescopic front forks a hydraulic damping system?

Most motor-cycle forks feature a damping system, but utility

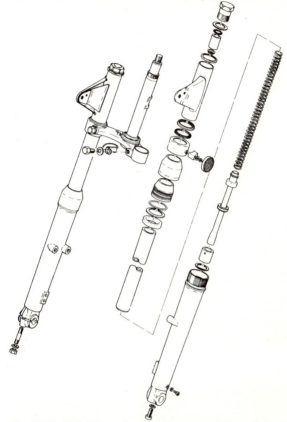

Fig. 24. Exploded view of a typical modern, oil-damped front fork assembly. This is a unit made by the Japanese Yamaha company for their range of two-stroke machines

mopeds simply use a spring, in some cases of variable pitch providing a progressive action.

What other types of front suspension is used?

Design trends have now all but eliminated the leading-or trailing-fork suspension system whereby the wheel is mounted on a hoop extending either around the front or the rear of the front tyre.

What is the commonest form of rear suspension?

Many manufacturers now use a pivoting form with spring-and-hydraulic-damped units either side of the machine connected at their bottom ends to the fork at a point near the rear-wheels axle and at their tops to the rear sub-frame in the region of the rear of the dual seat.

The pivoting-fork assembly has only one serious drawback. As the suspension moves up and down the free play in the rear chain increases and decreases. This is becoming an increasing problem as manufacturers opt for longer and softer suspension set-ups.

Is there any way around this problem?

The problem has been solved, at some considerable expense on some competition machines which have an intermediate pair of sprockets between the final drive and the rear wheel, mounted so as to use the swinging-fork pivot point as their centre. This necessitates the use of two chains and a considerable bearing mounting problem where the double sprocket runs on the swinging-arm pivot.

Is there any other way of combating chain-tension difficulties?

With competition machines, particularly those in use in trials, where very great amounts of rear wheel movement are used, a tensioner has been introduced on the lower chain run and this may well become the vogue for road machines.

Can motor-cycle suspension systems be adjusted?

Front forks are normally non-adjustable except by replacing

the internal springs with those of a heavier or a lighter rating or increasing or decreasing the viscosity of the damping fluid.

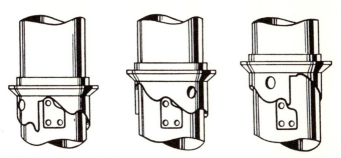

Fig. 25. Spring pre-load can be adjusted on most rear suspension units by turning the cammed sleeve on which the bottom of the spring is located. In the drawing on the left the spring is in its minimum pre-load condition. In the middle it is in its half-way setting position while on right the spring is set for maximum pre-load

Most rear suspension systems, however, provide for a degree of adjustment by varying the pre-load tension of the springs.

STEERING

What factors contribute to the good or bad steering of a machine?

Many points must be considered with respect to the steering geometry of a two-wheeled vehicle. Assuming that the basic design is sound, the variables which will affect steering will include the following: condition and inflation of the tyres, adjustment of the headstock spindle where the front forks are attached to the main frame, alignment of the wheels, satisfactory action of the front and rear suspension, the type of handlebars used. Some mention has already been made in this chapter about the problems of tyres and suspension.

How can headstock-spindle adjustment be made?

The majority of front forks are mounted in two yokes, the lower one having a fixed spindle which mounts through the headstock of the frame. The top yoke is then lowered over the two fork stanchions and the headstock and clamped into place by means of two nuts. Adjustment is made by tightening the lower nut until there is no free play in the bearings and yet there is no tightness or stickiness as the forks are moved over their full travel. The top nut is then used to lock its mate into position.

How can wheel alignment be checked?

It is possible to check wheel alignment scientifically by placing

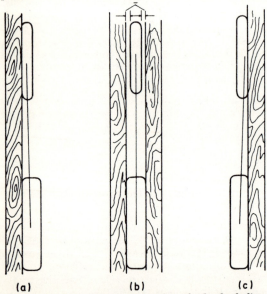

Fig. 26. Straight edges can be used to check wheel alignment. In (a) the front wheel is set too far to the left. The converse is true in (c). Only in (b) is the alignment correct with the front wheel set centrally between the two faces

straight edges along the rear tyre and measuring the offset of the front wheel against them. However, a far more satisfactory system, and this is part of racing practice, is to check the alignment by eye. Standing with your back to the rear of the machine and 3 m (10 ft.) away from it, bend down and sight the rear wheel through your legs. It will then be easy to see whether the rear wheel is in line with the axis of the machine and whether the front wheel is offset either to the left or to the right.

If the machine is properly assembled how can the wheels then go out of alignment?

Rear chain adjustment of most machines is effected by moving the rear wheel backwards and forwards in the slots provided at the end of the pivoting fork. If great care is not taken to ensure that the spindle moves backwards or forwards exactly the same amount at each side, misalignment will occur. It can be corrected by re-adjustment of the chain tensioning bolts.

Front wheels seldom go out of alignment but this can be caused by poor assembly of the components and spacers, for example, after a brake check.

Are the low, clip-on racing-type handlebars an aid to steering?

The prime reason for handlebars being mounted at a low position on a racing machine is so that the rider can lay his chest and chin on the fuel tank and provide a minimum frontal area and therefore less wind resistance.

This is not a consideration with road machines and it will be found that low, narrow handlebars contribute to a great deal of lack of control at low speeds.

Do the high-rise chopper-type handlebars aid or mar control?

There is no mechanical reason why the distance of the handlebars from the top fork yoke should make any difference to control but, in fact, the leverage set up by the 'ape hanger' type of bar on the handlebar mounting is so large that the clasping action is insufficient to deal with the load subjected upon it by the movements.

7
ELECTRICAL SYSTEMS

What systems are used to generate electricity on a motor cycle?

The d.c. brush-type dynamos have all but disappeared from use and the vast majority of motor cycles use an a.c. alternator for generating electrical current. The current produced from the alternator - normally mounted with its rotor on the crankshaft - is used, via a d.c. rectifier, to charge the machine's battery. Current is then drawn from the battery for ignition lighting, starting and hooter requirements.

What are the legal lighting requirements for motor cycles in Britain?

Any headlamp with a bulb exceeding 7 W must be capable of being dipped so as not to dazzle persons standing more than 7.6 m (25 ft.) ahead and having an eye level of less than 1.068 m (3½ ft).

In addition to a rear lamp which must have a bulb of a power not less than 6 W, all solos must have one red reflector.

On sidecar machines two rear lamps and two reflectors must be fitted. The reflectors must be at the same height and the rear lamps have the same appearance when illuminated. Moreover, they must be wired so that the failure of one would not prevent the other being lit.

Is it legal to use a machine to which lights are not fitted?

There are various interpretations of the law on this point. However, it is generally accepted that, provided the machine has no form of lighting whatsoever, then it may legally be ridden on the road during daylight hours. However, if any form of lighting set is fitted to the machine - and some authorities hold that even part of a wiring harness could be interpreted as part of a lighting set - it must be in full working order.

What maintenance is necessary on lighting equipment on a motor cycle?

Faced with the design problems, particularly those of space and styling, motor-cycle engineers have produced machines on which the battery has difficulty in coping with the demands of the electrical system.

In a car there is sufficient space in the under bonnet or the boot compartments to house a battery of more than

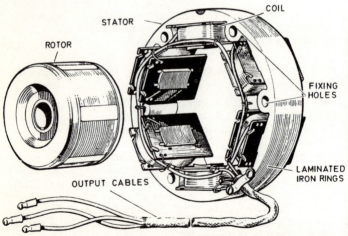

Fig. 27. The Lucas alternator. The stator is mounted on the crankcase with the rotor mounted on the crankshaft

adequate size. But a motor-cycle designer has no such easy way out.

Therefore maintenance and care of the battery, if it is to give its best, is at a premium.

Motor-cycle batteries also suffer from considerably more vibration than do their car counterparts.

Great care should be taken when mounting the battery to ensure that any protective rubber vibration-damping material is in place and that the battery strap is secure but not over-tight.

Considerable amounts of current can be wasted through bad connections which should periodically be removed from the battery and cleaned.

Alternators and rectifiers need no specific regular maintenance, only a periodic check, when convenient, to ensure that they are mounted securely.

How should a battery be charged?

A motor-cycle battery, as said earlier, is a delicate affair and no attempt should be made to force-charge the unit.

A maximum charging rate of 2 A should be used on any small-capacity battery and a regular check kept on the level of the electrolite.

8

ROUTINE MAINTENANCE

What regular maintenace is necessary for a motor cycle?

It is impossible to lay down hard-and-fast rules for the amount of maintenance necessary to keep a motor cycle in order. The degree of work necessary depends on the age of the machine, the type of work which it is being asked to do and the way in which it is driven. Climatic conditions also play a part in determining how trouble free a motor cycle will be.

However, it is possible to evolve a system based on distance which should result in trouble-free riding if sufficient diligence is paid to the maintenance tasks involved. Despite the fact that different machines with different types of engines have varied maintenance needs, it is possible to lay down some rules with the proviso that rarely-used machines in temperate climates may require less than the suggested minimum, other machines which suffer a hard life, perhaps are garaged in the open, will need more than the average amount of maintenance.

What are the absolute essentials?

Regular checks should be made on the oil tank on four-stroke machines and on two-stroke machines with a separate oiling system. Regular checks should also be made on tyre pressures.

Can you suggest a maintenance schedule for 1500 kilometre intervals?

With a machine that consumes little oil between maintenance inspections, the lubricant should be changed and all filters,

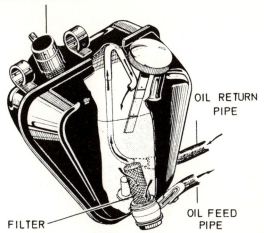
Fig. 28. A four-stroke oil tank with its filter on the feed pipe

whether in the oil tank, the engine or in both, should be thoroughly cleaned. Machines which consume, because of age, large quantities of oil, need not have the lubricant completely changed at such regular intervals but the filters should be checked and cleaned.

Two-stroke machines with separate oiling systems and therefore an oil reservoir need not have the lubricant changed as, unlike the four-stroke, it has not circulated the engine. The oil level in the primary-transmission chamber should be checked and the level brought up to that recommended by the manufacturer.

Although with the advent of sealed bearings, less grease nipples are now featured on modern machines, any in use should be greased with a gun at this 1500 kilometre interval. At the same time all pivot points at handlebar levers, rear-brake pedal etc., should be lightly oiled and the excess wiped away.

The air cleaner should be inspected and if necessary cleaned as detailed in Chapter Four.

Sparking plugs should be removed, cleaned with a wire brush and the gap re-set to the manufacturer's recommendation.

Check free play in the rear chain which, if necessary, should be adjusted to the limits set in the manufacturer's

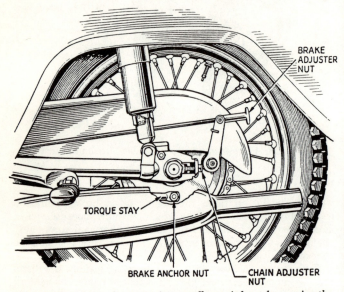

Fig. 29. Rear chain adjustment is normally carried out by moving the rear wheel but be sure that the movement is carried out equally at each side of the wheel

handbook. New chains initially need considerable adjustment but after a settling-in period this should only be necessary at this 1500 kilometre interval.

On machines with no chain-oiling facility, the chain should be removed, cleaned in paraffin, dried, and greased with a special chain lubricant before re-assembling.

Free movement of the front-brake lever and the rear-brake foot pedal should be checked and adjustment made if necessary. Also, check adjustment of the free play of the clutch lever which should move about 0.5 cm (3/16 in) at the nipple position.

Check that the battery terminals are tight, that the battery is secure in its housing and that the acid level is correct. If the level is low it should be topped up to the mark indicated on the casing - or about 0.03 cm (1/8 in) above the plates where no mark is provided - with distilled water, available from most garages, or with water recovered when defrosting a refrigerator or freezer.

What maintenance requirements are there at longer distance intervals?

At 5000 kilometre intervals the contact-breaker points on machines not fitted with electronic, point-less ignition systems should be cleaned and adjusted to manufacturer's recommendations. After the points have been re-set, the ignition timing should be checked and, if necessary re-set.

Tappet adjustment should be carried out, setting the clearances to the recommended limits. The same procedure should be followed in tightening the tension of the primary chain where fitted and the camshaft chain on machines using a chain-driven, overhead camshaft and without the provision of an automatic tensioner.

At this distance interval both brakes should be dismantled and inspected for wear.

A general inspection of the whole machine should be carried out and should include checking the tightness of all bolts and nuts not forgetting those used to mount accessories.

The carburettor should be cleaned to remove any sediment which has collected in the float chamber. On many machines it is possible to perform this task without removing the complete carburettor from the cylinder head.

When are more major items checked out?

An interval of 20 000 km is suggested for the major item of

lifting the cylinder head and inspecting the combustion chamber.

On four-stroke engines, the valves should also be removed and inspected. Regardless of whether new valves are fitted or the old items re-used, they should be ground to provide an air-tight seal, using a combination of fine and course grinding paste until a point of contact can be seen around the complete valve face and the face of the valve seat. Ideally, the inlet valve should have a thin contact line to prevent too much heat transfer from the combustion chamber to the valve. A wider contact line is permissible with the exhaust valve.

Also on four-stroke engines, the free length of the valve

Fig. 30. The comparison between a worn and an unused valve spring. The spring on the left has compressed in use well below the manufacturer's limits and should be replaced

springs should be checked and if these have compressed in use below the minimum laid down by the manufacturer, they should be replaced with new items.

Is this top overhaul mandatory at the 20 000 kilometre interval?

Such an overhaul is normally determined by a fall-off in engine performance and condition and may well occur before or after the 20 000 kilometre mark suggested.

Is it worth removing the cylinder for a piston and piston-ring inspection at the same time?

Again this depends on the general performance and feel of the engine. On motors where lifting the cylinders to reveal the pistons and rings is very little extra work, there is no reason

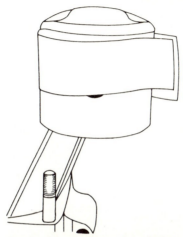

Fig. 31. When replacing the cylinder, a simple ring clamp can be made up from a short length of alloy or tin-plate scrap

why this cannot be done at the same time. However, if it is felt that a simple de-coke and valve grind will restore the pep of the power unit, lifting of the cylinder may be left until the 40 000 kilometre interval.

Do the same rules apply to a two-stroke engine?

Cylinder heads and cylinders of two-stroke engines should be lifted at the 20 000 kilometre interval so that excess carbon may be removed from the combustion chamber, the piston and the exhaust ports of the cylinder itself.

Recent advances in oil technology have reduced the amount of carbon produced by a two-stroke engine and a 20 000 kilometre interval is now considered sufficient for such an operation.

How should carbon be removed?

Rules are the same for four- and two-stroke engines. Great care is necessary so as not to score the cylinder head face or the top of the piston. However, old-time hints that a piece of

Fig. 32. An ideal tool for clearing carbon deposits from piston ring grooves is a section of old ring but be sure that any sharp edges do not score the piston material

wood or solder should be used to rub away the carbon are ineffectual and the deposit should be removed, with care, using a blunt screwdriver or similar 'gentle' instrument.

What else is necessary at the 20 000 kilometre interval?

The ignition timing should be checked using ideally an electronic strobe for the best results.

The steering head bearings should be checked for free play and adjusted if necessary, and the oil drained from the telescopic forks. New oil of the correct viscosity rating should be added as recommended by the manufacturer.

Particularly on large-capacity machines the rear chain may have worn beyond a point where adjustment is no longer possible and, unless replacement is made, the teeth of the rear wheel and gearbox sprockets may suffer. A good general rule for checking chain conditions is to remove the item from the machine and lay it on the garage floor. Carefully compress the chain link by link to shorten it to its minimum length. Then measure the chain. Now elongate it by holding

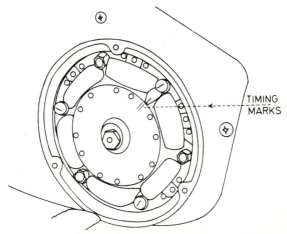

Fig. 33. Timing marks are usually provided by the manufacturer to enable accurate ignition timing to be carried out with a strobe

one end and pulling the other. Again measure. If the difference between the compressed and stretched measurements is over 2.2 cm (7/8 in) the chain should be replaced by a new item.

What other routine maintenance tasks are likely to be necessary?

Other possible maintenance needs cannot be determined by engine life as such items as re-boring the cylinders, replacing big-ends and main bearings, will become evident either by a drastic falling off in performance or from foreign mechanical noise in the engine.

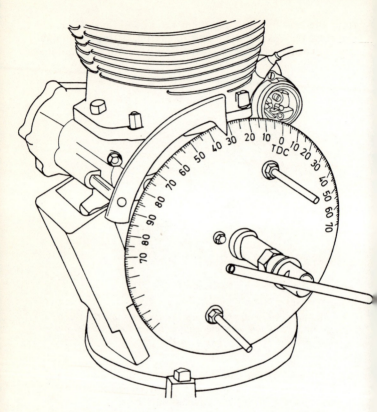

Fig. 34. An engine timing disc in use on a twin-cylinder Norton

What tools are necessary for motor-cycle maintenance?

With the increase in sophistication of the motor cycle, more and more special tools, designed specifically for maintenance work, are required for major repair tasks.

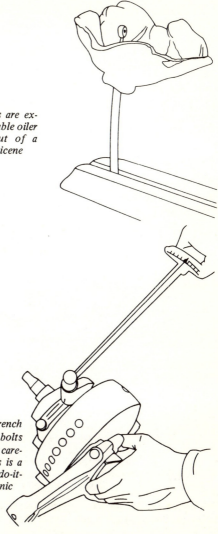

Fig. 35. Not all tools are expensive. This simple cable oiler can be fashioned out of a small piece of plasticene

Fig. 36. A torque wrench by which nuts and bolts can be tightened to carefully controlled limits is a must for the serious do-it-yourself bike mechanic

However, a large amount of routine maintenance can be done by an enthusiast with a reasonable collection of hand tools.

It is suggested that a minimum tool kit should consist of a set of open-ended spanners of the sizes used for the particular type of machine owned. This should be supplemented with a set of ring spanners, screwdrivers with cross-head and straight points in at least three sizes, two pairs of pilers, one with a pointed nose, one with a flat nose and cutting facility, and a soft-headed hammer or mallet.

How do I know the sizes of spanners necessary for my machine?

Japanese and European-made machines use nuts with metric-size heads and therefore a set of metric spanners is necessary. Until a short time ago most British machines had nuts with

Fig. 37. When removing the gearbox-mainshaft nut, the final drive sprocket can be held by a tool made from a short length of chain bolted to a steel strip

Whitworth-size heads but currently most are being produced either with metric heads or with American AF sizes.

Unfortunately, some Triumph machines were actually produced with a combination of Whitworth and AF head-size nuts and bolts.

Is a socket set necessary?

A socket set is a great advantage and, with a good range of attachments, can almost take the place of a ring-spanner set and, when a ratchet is used, is obviously a great time and energy saver.

What specialist tooling is necessary for routine maintenance?

The trend is towards dealer servicing and dealer maintenance and many machines are designed with this in view. A major engine strip-down is becoming more and more outside the province of the average enthusiast.

Is there no way in which these tools can be obtained?

All tools can be purchased from respective companies but sheer cost rules out many of them for the one-machine owner. However, many owners' clubs purchase such tools and loan these to their members.

TROUBLE SHOOTING

What is the procedure for locating the fault if the engine fails to start?

It may seem obvious, but the first thing to do is to check that there is sufficient fuel in the petrol tank, and that the ignition is switched on.

If the tank has fuel, check that there is no obstruction in the petrol pipe or at the carburettor. On carburettors with a float-chamber tickler, we can ascertain whether there is fuel in the chamber by depressing the tickler. On models with other richening devices the float chamber may have to be removed to ensure that the fuel has reached it.

Another possible cause of non-starting may be a result of excessive or insufficient richening of the mixture when the engine is cold.

If the carburettor is overflooded, excess fuel will reach the sparking plug which may become too wet to ignite the mixture. This problem can sometimes be cured by switching off the fuel, opening the throttle wide and turning the engine over a dozen times. If this does not cure the problem, the sparking plug must be removed and dried or replaced with another item.

When an engine is cold it needs an excess of fuel to enable it to start and insufficient flooding of the carburettor or richening of the mixture by means of the starting lever, depending upon the type of carburettor fitted, will prevent the engine coming to life.

If the fuel system seems to be operating well, what is the next point to check?

Now move on to the ignition system and the quickest check is to remove the sparking plug, re-attach it to a high tension cable and then lay the plug on the cylinder head so that the metal body of the sparking plug is in firm contact with the engine. Now spin the engine over and a clear spark should be seen to jump the gap between the earth wire and the centre electrode. If no spark occurs make the check again with an alternative sparking plug which is known to be in good order. If this plug produces the desired spark it can be fitted and the malfunctioning plug either cleaned or scrapped.

If no spark is evident with either plug one must look deeper for the cause of the problem.

On machines with contact-breaker points, check that the points are opening and closing and that they are in a clean condition. On coil-ignition machines check that the battery is not exhausted. Many modern machines have a fuse protecting the ignition circuit and this can be checked to ensure that it has not blown.

Are there any other possible reasons why this machine should not start?

The more usual and basic reasons have been dealt with. Other possibilities are that crankcase seals in a two-stroke engine have failed or that ignition timing has slipped or, on a four-stroke engine, that the valve timing has gone awry.

What should be checked if the engine fails to start or misfires after wet weather?

Water can have reached three places which will cause this problem.

It is possible that water has entered the carburettor in which case it should be dismantled and dried. Water may have entered the contact-breaker assembly in which case it should be cleaned out with particular attention paid to contact-breaker points themselves. However, the more likely cause of this malady is that moisture is allowing the high tension spark to track through the outside wiring at the ignition coil or plug cover. Again these should be dried out.

What if the same misfiring symptoms are evident in dry weather?

Here the fault can be the result of a restricted flow of fuel, poor carburettor adjustment or a defect in the ignition system.

What form is the ignition defect likely to take?

It could be a defective condenser which would be evident from a steady intense spark across the contact-breaker points and bad pitting of the points themselves. The same symptoms would manifest themselves if the contact-breaker points were dirty or out of adjustment. Other possible causes are dirty or poorly-set sparking plugs or bad connections in the h.t. lead where it joins the coil or the sparking-plug terminal.

If performance drops off radically what should be checked?

Apart from the items mentioned above, the problem could be caused by a dirty air cleaner, the malfunctioning of the ignition automatic advance or an obstruction at the carburettor main jet.

On a four-stroke engine, other causes of lack of performance are the closing up of the tappet clearances, valves sticking due to gummed-up stems, failure of the piston or excessive wear in the piston rings.

Is the same true of two-stroke engines?

Piston ring condition is very critical on a two-stroke engine and so too is the state of the crankshaft engine seals on which the degree of primary compression depends.

Is there any way to test for lack of compression?

A test may be carried out by simply turning over the engine on the kick starter and feeling the resistance. Lack of resistance on a four-stroke engine will either indicate broken piston rings, an extremely worn bore or bad seating of the valves. On a two-stroke engine it will be either badly worn or broken piston rings, a worn bore or failure of the crankcase seals.

A more scientific test may be carried out using a pressure gauge mounted in the plug hole which will give an indication of the psi built up in the combustion chamber. This can be checked against the manufacturer's figures.

The only other possible cause of a drastic lack of compression would be a leaking joint between the cylinder head and the cylinder itself. However, this will be easily heard as a whistling noise whenever the engine is cranked.

How can one diagnose engine faults by ear?

Before attempting to diagnose any engine noise, first check the most likely cause. On many machines this is excessive play or wear in the primary drive chain or overhead camshaft drive chain.

A sharp pinging noise when accelerating at low engine rev/min is caused by detonation. This is a fault of over-advanced ignition timing or too low a grade of fuel.

A heavy metallic knock is usually a result of a failed big-end bearing and should be investigated immediately.

A deep rumble is most likely to be caused by a worn crankshaft bearing or one loose in its housing. A mechanical knock when accelerating can be caused by excessive piston slap because of a worn piston and/or bore or a small-end worn in the con-rod eye.

What are the causes of excessive oil consumption?

On a two-stroke engine with separate oiling system and an engine-driven pump, the fault will lie with the setting of the pump or the pump mechanism itself.

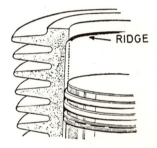

Fig. 38. The point of maximum wear on a piston is on the section just below the ridge indicated

On a four-stroke engine, excessive oil consumption is a result of worn or broken piston rings, a worn cyclinder bore or excessive wear in the valve or valve guides.

When do cylinders need re-boring?

Heavy oil consumption and mechanical noise from a slapping piston will normally indicate the need for a re-bore. Sometimes it is possible to simply install a new set of piston rings but before this is done bore wear should be measured at a point just below the lip which forms at the top of the cylinder. If this is more than 0.017 cm (0.007 in) a re-bore is probably indicated. This measurement should be carried out with an internal micrometer or a Mercer gauge and a comparison made

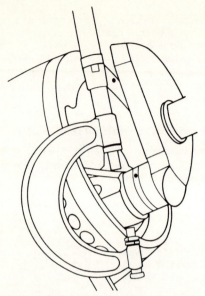

Fig. 39. A workshop foreman will use an external micrometer to measure wear on big-end journals

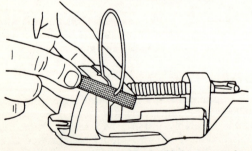

Fig. 40. If piston rings need to be filed to ensure that the gap is as recommended by the engine manufacturer, the body of the ring itself should be firmly held to prevent breakage

between the cylinder bore at three points - at the highest point of ring travel (as above), at a point mid-way down the cylinder and at the lowest possible point in the cylinder where wear is at a minimum.

Because of the thrust action of the piston, wear is never uniform and measurements should be taken in line and across the axis of the machine.

To what size should the engine be re-bored?

Measuring the cylinder bore should tell an engineer just what size the aperture will have to be bored before it is again completely concentric throughout its length. Although pistons are often available in oversizes of 0.025 cm (0.010 in), 0.050 cm (0.020 in), 0.075 cm (0.030 in) and 0.010 cm (0.040 in) it is obviously advisable to use the smallest possible size so that further re-bores may be made if necessary.

9
LICENSING, INSURANCE, LEGAL NOTES

LICENSING

What is the earliest age at which a person may ride a moped or a motor cycle?

Generally a lower age limit is described for moped riding than for motor cycle or car use. In Britain, for example, a moped may be used by a rider 16 years old. Motor-cycle legislation requires the rider to be one year older.

What form of licence is necessary?

In Britain a provisional licence must be initially taken out. This allows a rider to use his machine provided that L-plates are fixed to the front and rear.

A full licence can be obtained after a driving test has been taken and passed.

The holder of a provisional licence may not ride a machine of over 250 cc until he has passed a motor-cycle driving test.

Are moped and motor-cycle tests the same?

No. A person who has passed a test for a motor cycle is also deemed to have a full licence in respect of a moped. But the reverse is not true.

Therefore a person who takes and passes a moped test must also take a test for a motor cycle.

Some motor cycles and mopeds have automatic gearboxes. Are there separate classes for these as for cars?

There is no distinction between automatic and manual-transmission two wheelers.

May a learner rider carry a passenger?

Until he has passed a test, the holder of a provisional licence may not take a passenger on a solo motor cycle unless that passenger has full licence to cover that category of machine.

Is the same true for a sidecar outfit?

No. A learner on a sidecar outfit may take a passenger regardless of his qualifications.

What is the situation for mopeds?

The same as for solo motor cycles. However few mopeds allow for pillion passengers and the law dictates that a machine must have a properly constructed seat and foot-rests for a pillion passenger if one is to be carried. Because of the limited power of most mopeds, they are generally unsuitable for pillion work.

How is excise duty assessed in Great Britain?

Current legislation in Britain has three classes of excise duty for motor cycles. They are for machines of up to 150 cc, for 150 to 250 cc and for over 250 cc.

For machines of up to 150 cc the duty is £4 per year: for 150 to 250 cc, £8: and for over 250 cc, £16.

Licences above a subscribed minimum level can currently be purchased for three-month periods. In these the total cost of the four three-month licences exceed the annual fee.

Current legislation does not differentiate between solo and sidecar machines. Both are liable to the same amount of taxation, dependent on engine size.

INSURANCE

What insurance is necessary?

Various countries insist on different levels of insurance cover. However, the British system is typical of most in that the minimum cover required by law is third-party insurance whereby anyone who suffers from your negligence can claim from your insurance company. It also provides for passenger liability. However, most companies are reluctant to quote for this minimum cover and nearly always consider third party, fire and theft, with passenger cover as the minimum they will accept as an insurance risk.

What cover does this give?

The third-party insurance covers against claims by any party on foot or in another vehicle which may come about through any accident for which the insured may be held to blame.
　Passenger liability covers against similar claims which may be made by a pillion or sidecar passenger. Fire and theft cover provides insurance in case the machine is stolen or suffers in a fire.

Is there a more all-embracing insurance which will cover loss or damage in an accident where no third party is involved?

Yes. This is called fully-comprehensive cover and premiums are obviously more expensive than for lesser risks.

Does this mean that one would receive a new machine if an insured motor cycle was stolen or written off by fire or accident?

Very unlikely. Firstly, many companies require the insured to pay the first so many pounds of each claim - to avoid encouraging trivial claims - and, secondly, the company will only, in most cases, pay out the current market value of a machine, not the price of a replacement.

This means that the amount paid out is what an owner would expect to receive for a model if sold to a dealer, not the price that a customer would have to pay.

May one choose whatever cover is most suitable?

Normally, yes. However many finance companies may insist on a form of comprehensive insurance if they have an interest in the machine.

How are premiums assessed?

Many factors including a rider's age, experience, accident record, employment and place of residence will affect that premiums as well as the size of the machine, its value, and availability and price of replacement parts.

Are no-claims-bonuses allowed?

Yes, but not to the same extent as for cars. Most companies average a top no-claims-bonus of around 20%, earned after three years without a claim.

LEGAL NOTES

Are motor cycles liable for roadworthiness tests in the same way as cars?

Yes. In Britain, for example, machines over three years old must be tested and a pass certificate granted each year.

Where can the tests be carried out?

Many motor-cycle dealers are registered as testing stations and they will examine machines. An appointment is usually necessary.

What happens if the machine is re-submitted after a failure?

A scale of charges dependent upon the number of parts to be repaired or replaced has been laid down and it is generally cheaper, if the work has to be done by a garage, to have it carried out by the company who initially tested the machine. Parts of the machine which have already been tested and passed will not then have to be re-tested and therefore an eventual pass certificate will be cheaper.

What items are actually tested?

The registered tester has to satisfy himself that the brakes, tyres, lights and steering are in good order but he can decline to test the machine if it has any other basic faults which make it unroadworthy. He can also refuse to test a machine if it is too dirty or has insufficient fuel for the test to be carried out satisfactorily.

May one solo motor cycle tow another vehicle?

The law varies from country to country on this point but in Britain the solo motor cycle may only tow another solo, sidecar, or three-wheeler that has broken down.

Can a trailer be towed?

Again various countries have different laws, and in Britain a solo may not tow a trailer. But a sidecar outfit can be used to tow a trailer provided that the trailer meets with certain legal requirements. Maximum permissible length is 6.9 m (22 ft.).

Must a rider wear a safety helmet?

Yes. There are no exceptions to the rule on medical, religious or any other grounds. All motor-cycle riders and passengers, except those in a sidecar, must wear an approved helmet and it must be securely fastened.

May an auxiliary spot lamp be fitted to a machine?

Yes, but there are restrictions. Unless it is used only in conditions of snow or fog, a lamp exceeding 7 W must not be less than 61 cm (24 in) above the ground.

Can a fibre-glass or plastic fuel tank be fitted to a machine?

In Britain machines first used after July 1, 1973, and not manufactured before February 1, 1973, must be fitted with metal fuel tanks.

Are there any other legal restrictions specific to powered two-wheelers?

The rider of a two-wheeled solo machine must not carry more than one passenger and that passenger must sit astride the machine.

In parking meter zones machines may only be parked in specially-marked motor-cycle parking areas.

Motor cycles under 50 cc and mopeds are not allowed to use motorways.

10
ON THE ROAD

RIDING A MOTOR CYCLE

How should a newcomer learn to ride a machine?

Ideally the first venture on two wheels should be made in the most secluded spot available.

If it is possible to use a car park or any area where there is no traffic, this will be ideal for it is important, first of all, to learn to use the clutch so that smooth getaways can be accomplished.

What are the secrets of safe riding?

There are no secrets as such. A safe rider is a confident rider. He is not conspicuous in traffic and is at ease on his machine. To achieve this he must have controls set to suit him so that any action he may have to take while riding the machine does not involve an unnatural movement. This relaxed riding position leads to better control of the machine and, of course, reduces tiredness, itself one of the enemies of good riding.

The important thing is to progress slowly, to ride initially within your limitations until a thorough rapport has been established between rider and machine.

Do wet road surfaces call for different riding techniques?

The only problem occasioned by wet road surfaces is a reduction in the friction between tyre and surface. This means that all movements including cornering, braking and accelerating must be made in a more gentle and progressive manner if the all-important traction is not to be lost.

At what times are road surfaces most dangerous?

During a dry spell oil and rubber from car tyres are deposited on the road surface. As soon as rain starts, a thin film of water spreads over these deposits and makes the surface very slippery. Therefore, it is immediately after rain has started that roads are at their most hazardous. With heavy rain the deposits are washed away and the degree of grip which the tyre will have on the road is simply dependent upon the state of the tyres and the road surface.

Are some road surfaces better than others?

Concrete has very good grip in the wet but other surfaces, particularly cobbles, are always a hazard when wet.

How should braking be accomplished in slippery conditions?

In dry weather on good roads the majority of braking is done with the front wheel because weight transferred to the front of the machine makes this the most effective brake. However, a front wheel skid in the wet is a very difficult thing to control and many riders prefer to use their rear brake more in damp conditions as a rear wheel skid can easily be brought under control.

In slippery conditions the important thing is to allow plenty of time and space to brake gently, smoothly, and progressively.

RIDING A SIDECAR OUTFIT

Are there special techniques for driving sidecar outfits?

The sidecar is something of an anachronism. It has been said that it does not steer, does not stop, has all the disadvantages of a car, all the disadvantages of a motor cycle and none of the attributes of either.

This is, perhaps, too cynical an appraisal and although, with the current levelling out of costs between cars and motor cycles, the sidecar is not the economical family transport it once was, it has a large following amongst sporting riders who are happy to accept its unique challenges.

The main problem is that although a solo is quite happy to be banked over and turn corners, a sidecar outfit has to be driven with different techniques for left or right corners.

What is the technique for a left-hand corner?

Assume that the sidecar is mounted, British fashion, on the left. The driving wheel is at the right and the sidecar wheel is doing nothing on the left other than providing drag. This, in effect means, that to turn a left-hand corner the rear wheel must be driven at a faster speed than the sidecar wheel. This is best achieved by approaching the corner at a slower speed than the bend would normally demand, and then gently accelerating the machine around it.

Does the same hold true for right-hand corners?

The converse is true. On right-hand corners with a left-hand sidecar, the driven rear wheel of the motor cycle needs to turn at a slower speed than the sidecar wheel which is completing a larger arc to make the bend. Therefore, the corner is entered at a slightly faster speed and either the throttle closed as the turn is made or even the brakes gently applied.

On Continental and American sidecar outfits, the sidecar is fitted to the right-hand side. What is the procedure in these cases?

The reverse of the British cornering technique is applicable. With the sidecar mounted on the right, the sidecar should be accelerated gently around right-hand corners and decelerated around left-hand corners.

Are there any particular dangers attached to learning to drive a sidecar outfit?

Most of the problems attached to driving a sidecar outfit are psychological but nevertheless very real to the driver.

A novice driver sitting on a machine with an empty sidecar immediately senses that all the weight is on his side of the machine and that the sidecar is riding light. On a left-hand corner, with a left-hand-mounted sidecar, a sidecar will naturally tend to lift and tip. If no correction is made to this tendency the machine will keel over and the natural reaction of a rider will be to turn the handlebars to the right and shoot the bike over to the opposite side of the road. This is how the majority of sidecar accidents occur.

Even if the sidecar wheel does not actually lift, there is the worrying feeling that it is about to. Again the rider tends to freeze and will fail to complete the turn.

How can the novice rider overcome this?

By far the best method is to weigh the sidecar down. Toolboxes, old batteries, anvils, scrap iron - almost anything can be used. As a rider becomes more efficient, the weight can be slowly reduced.

Once proficiency on a sidecar has been achieved it is possible to ride the outfit at quite breathtaking speeds around left-or right-hand corners without any weight in the sidecar.

RIDING EQUIPMENT

Is special riding equipment necessary for a motor cycle?

Dealing with riding suits first, it is extremely unwise, even in the warmest weather to ride a motor cycle without some form of protective clothing. A small spill at 10 or 15 km/h, which can be completely innocuous if the rider is wearing a light-weight riding suit, can turn into a nasty accident with considerable lacerations and grazes if the rider is taking too much advantage of fine weather and wearing only a pair of shorts and a tee-shirt.

What sort of riding suits are available?

Up to a few years ago the majority of riding suits were dull, drab affairs either composed of wax-proofed linen or rather unpliable plastic material.

However, increased use of nylon and more-pliable plastic materials has resulted in a new generation of riding gear. The drab black suit is now almost a thing of the past, and gaily-coloured riding gear is now the order of the day.

What are the pros and cons of these suits?

The waxed-linen suit was considerably more pliable than the plastic variety but it needed regular waxing of its waterproof qualities were to be retained and it tended to be dirty in use - its wax proofing was liable to rub off and leave marks on any light surface. The plastic suits were much more waterproof but tended to be uncomfortable to wear and eventually suffered from cracks after long use.

Research by road safety laboratories has shown that one of the main causes of accidents involving motor cycles is the failure of the motorists to see the relatively small frontal area of the motor cyclist who is about to overtake. Brightly-coloured suits therefore have the added advantage of calling attention to other road users of the presence of the motor cyclist. The clean-looking bright colours have also tended to make the motor cyclist more acceptable in restaurants, hotels, and cinemas, etc.

Will one suit do for all weathers?

In dry conditions a light-weight nylon oversuit is ideal, especially if worn during cold weather with warm undergarments.

In wet weather one of the modern plastic-based suits not only provides extra protection against the cold but are, nowadays, 100% waterproof.

Are crash helmets essential?

Crash helmets are now mandatory by law in Britain, and what is more they have to be of sufficient quality to receive a British Standards Institute certificate. When touring in certain foreign countries it is still possible to ride without a safety helmet but modern helmets are comfortable, well fitting, reasonably priced and there can be no real excuse for the risk involved in riding without this very necessary measure of protection.

What types of helmets are available?

There are three main categories of helmet. There is the so-called 'pudding basin' which is shaped as its name suggests. This has almost been superseded by the 'space-type' helmet which gives protection to the temples and to the base of the skull. The third type of helmet is an extension of the 'space-type' and is built with a larger degree of protection for the face, having a band around the chin and a porthole type opening at the front for the eyes and nose.

What are the advantages of these various types?

The pudding-basin type of helmet now has little advantage and has been outlawed for use in speed competitions by the Auto-Cycle Union. Of the two remaining helmet types, experts are still arguing the advisability of the full-face helmet, some claiming that, in the event of an accident, it is more difficult to remove and can, in some cases cause asphyxiation, by blocking off the mouth and nose.

Both types of helmets are extremely efficient and the evidence does suggest that the full-face helmet gives a greater degree of protection. However, because of the larger amount of materials involved, and the need for better fitting, these helmets tend to be more expensive.

What types of eye protection are available?

Eye protectors fall into two categories, goggles and face masks. Face masks can only be used with the 'space' or full-face helmets. With these types of helmet it is sometimes difficult to find a pair of goggles which fit comfortably within the framework of the helmet and therefore the advantage comes out clearly in favour of the face mask. However these masks are made of plastic and can easily scratch.

Should tinted masks be used?

Tinted masks should not be used in anything but the brightest sunlight. Many accidents have been attributed to the use of tinted masks in poor light.

What types of goggles are available?

Some goggles have a single transparent area, others are divided with one lens for each eye. Normal glass lenses should never be used. In the event of an accident they are a serious danger. Goggle lenses should be made of either safety glass or plastic.
   Safety glass has the advantage in that it does not scratch as easily as plastic but, is, of course, more expensive to replace.

How can goggle misting be prevented?

There are several proprietary compounds which can be applied to the inside of the goggles to prevent misting during rain. However many riders simply spread saliva on the inside of the goggles and this seems to work as well, if for a shorter period, than the special chemicals produced.

Are boots essential for motor cycling?

Boots, like clothing, afford a degree of protection. However, full-length motor-cycle boots are not always necessary although it is normally considered dangerous for a rider to wear a pair of plimsoles as these would afford no protection whatsoever in case of a brush with a car or even a low-speed fall.

Should gloves or gauntlets always be worn?

Protection is the keynote and some form of hand covering is necessary.

Because they have fewer seams, gauntlets are usually much more weatherproof than gloves but they do tend to afford a lesser degree of finesse with controls. Many experienced riders opt for a pair of supply, light-weight leather gloves and carry a pair of waterproof overmits which can be slipped over the gloves for use in wet weather.

ACCESSORIES

What accessories can be fitted to a motor cycle?

Until a short time ago very few accessories were offered as standard fittings on new machines. This was because of fierce competition between manufacturers and the desire for each to keep the basic price of their machines to a minimum.

However, during recent years such items as steering locks, helmet holders, rear-view mirrors, and winking turn-indicators have become standard. Many of the fitments are a result of American legislation which demands their fitting before machines can be imported into that country.

Should safety bars be fitted to machines?

Once in vogue, safety bars across the front of the machine to protect vital components in the event of a crash are now the exception rather than the rule. No manufacturers fit them as standard and many fitted during their in-fashion period were useless for the machine design did not enable a sufficiently firm fixing to be made.

About the only machine which will benefit from such a fixture at the present time is the BMW Opposed Twin. This machine's low cylinder heads, can suffer dramatically in the event of even a low-speed spill, and a scientifically designed and properly fitted crash bar can be give considerable protection.

Are luggage carriers and panniers provided as standard fitments?

Some moped manufacturers offer, as standard equipment, a small shopping basket and small carriers fixed on to the rear of the machine. For other mopeds and motor cycles, there are various proprietary ranges of pannier bags and boxes including a range designed to sit upon the tank top.

What is the best position to fit a receptacle for carrying luggage?

Ideally such a fitment should be fitted as low as possible and as near the centre line of the machine. However, this is not practical and perhaps the best method of carrying luggage is in pannier bags slung on either side of the rear wheel.

Obviously the panniers should be securely mounted with no chance of their coming loose or their mountings fouling the rear wheel or coming into contact with any moving suspension parts.

Also it is advisable to ensure that access to the rear wheel, for rear-chain adjustment is not impaired by the fitting of the accessories.

What are the pros and cons of fairings?

A well-made, well-fitting fairing on a moped or small-capacity machine is an ideal fitment for a commuter rider as it will afford considerable protection against adverse weather conditions.

For larger-capacity sports and touring machines they are not as popular for, although they do give a considerable degree of protection from the elements, and, in fact, if well designed, boost top speed by improving the air flow around the machine, they tend to accentuate engine noise, impair accessibility and are also very prone to damage in the event of a spill.

Can spot lamps be fitted to a motor cycle?

Provided that the law, which requires any spot lamp exceeding 7 W to be fitted not less than 60.9 cm (24 in) above the ground unless it is to be used only in conditions of fog or while snow is falling is complied with, there is no reason why spot lamps should not be fitted to augment the headlamp beam.

However a motor-cycle battery does not have tremendous reserves of power and the regular use of a large-wattage spot lamp will mean that a more rigorous check will have to be kept on the battery condition.

What other accessories are worthwhile?

Although the majority of machines are now fitted with fairly secure steering locks, this does not prevent the whole machine being lifted away and many riders are now using a stout padlock and chain to secure the machine to an immovable object when leaving it unattended for long periods.

SPORTING ACTIVITY

Can a standard road-going motor cycle be used for sporting activity?

There are a considerable number of sporting competitions which cater solely and specifically for road-going machines.

These range from local-council-organised road-safety contests where the rider has to negotiate a series of obstacles, answer queries on machine maintenance and on the highway code and perform a short observed road test to the annual Auto-Cycle Union national rally in which riders cover a 1000 kilometre course - or less depending upon their aspirations - calling at check points all over Britain.

Can a moped be used for such competitions?

Mopeds are regularly used in these types of contests. In fact, many competitions of this nature have special classes and awards for pedal-assisted machines.

Are there more ambitious events for motor-cycle owners?

Each year in Britain there are a large number of competitive and non-competitive rallies and events based upon map-reading and route-finding on public roads.

Do more serious forms of competition require specialist machinery?

Any form of riding in which speed plays a part now demands a fairly-specialised motor cycle.

Are there not classes for production machines in road racing?

It is possible to use standard road-going motor cycles in production races but usually these machines have been specifically tailored for the events.

What other forms of motor-cycle competition exist?

The main forms of specialised motor-cycle sport are trials riding, scrambling, grass-track and road racing.

What are motor-cycle trials?

Trials consist of running machines over natural obstacles, such as hills, through mud, stream beds, gulleys, etc. Marks are lost for putting feet to the ground, for stopping or for riding outside the boundaries of the 'section'.

What types of machines are used for trials?

The majority of current trials machines are two-strokes made in Spain and Japan with capacities between 170 cc and 350 cc. Trials machines have wide ratio gears to give an ideal gearing for each type of hazard, high ground clearance to enable obstacles such as tree roots to be overcome and large clearances between the wheels and mudguards to prevent the build-up of mud.

There is no speed aspect to pure trials riding which is perhaps the cheapest form of specialised competitive sport.

How does this differ from scrambling?

Scrambling consists of racing over a short, defined circuit, the first rider to finish being the winner.

How do scrambling machines differ from trials bikes?

Trials machines have engines designed for a wide spread of power whereas scrambling engines are built with maximum power as almost the sole requisite. They have closer ratio gearboxes to enable full engine power to be used at all speeds and, as the machines are used on specifically designated tracks, they do have the same strict measure of silencing enforced as do trials machines, which have to be registered for road use.

Do road-racing machines follow the same pattern?

Road racing is perhaps, the most specialised of all forms of motor-cycle sport. Road-racing machines tend to be more expensive and much more factory development work has gone into their production. Machines have been produced with eight cylinders, super-chargers and as many as 10 gears.

How does grass-track racing differ?

Where scrambles are held on hilly courses with jumps during which the machines are airborne for a considerable time, grass-track events normally take place on a near-oval circuit which is relatively smooth and where the corners are ridden by broadsiding the machines.

Are there any other forms of motor-cycle sport?

There are other fringe forms of competition including drag racing or sprinting, where acceleration from a standing start over a certain distance is the sole criteria, speedway racing over short shale oval tracks, racing on sand, hill climbing on dirt and tarmac surfaces and even motor-cycle football where teams manoeuvre a giant-sized ball.

How does one break into any branch of motor-cycle sport?

The only real way to find out about motor-cycle sport, particularly from a competitive point of view, is to join one of the clubs specialising in the particular branch of competition in which one is interested.

How can contact with these clubs be made?

The Auto-Cycle Union has lists of addresses of all British clubs and also publishes an annual handbook giving addresses and, in some cases, telephone numbers, of the club secretaries.

The address of the ACU is 31 Belgrave Square, SW1. Telephone number 01 235 7636.

At what age can a rider compete in competition?

Various countries have their own age limits for youth motor cycling but in Britain the minimum age for competition uner ACU auspices for any speed event is 16 years old. Below this age the rider must compete in events organised by the youth division of the ACU.

Riders from six to seven years old are classed as cadets, those from eight to 10 as juniors, from 11 to 13 as intermediates and from 14 to 16 as seniors.

The position is slightly different with grass-track racing where the cadet and junior limits are the same but intermediates are from 11 to 12 years old, class A seniors from 13 to 14 and class A1 seniors from 15 to 16.

Are there capacity limits for each class?

The capacity limits vary according to the type of competition. For scrambles, cadets are limited to 50 cc machines, juniors to 80 cc, intermediates to 100 cc if the machine is of foreign origin and 150 cc if it is British, and the seniors to 125 cc foreign and 200 cc British.

For trials, cadets are limited to 50 cc, juniors to 100 cc, intermediates to 150 cc, and seniors to 200 cc.

For grass-track racing, the cadet limit is 50 cc, junior

100 cc, intermediate 200 cc, and the seniors are sub-divided with the 13 to 14 year olds limited to 200 cc and the 15 to 16 year olds to 250 cc.

INDEX

Accessories, 103
    fairings, 104
    luggage carriers, 104
    panniers, 104
    safety bars, 103
    spot lamps, 104–105
Amal carburettor, 23–26
    Concentric, 23
    Monobloc, 26
Automatic gearbox, 54

Battery care, 71
Boots, 102
Bowed flange, 36–37
Brakes, 56
    disc, 58
    hydraulic, 58
    shoe-and-drum, 56
British machines, 9
Butted spokes, 60

Capacity classes, 1
Carbon removal, 78
Carburettors,
    adjustment, 36
    Amal, 23–26
        Concentric, 23
        Monobloc, 26
    bowed-flange, 36–37
    cleaning, 30
    faults, 36
    slide-operated-throttle, 23
    SU, 35
    synchronisation, 32–33
    types of, 23
    vacuum, 23, 34–35
Chain adjustment, 48
Chain drive, 54
Chain wear, 78
Clutch linings, 53
Clutch springs, 53
Clutch systems, 51
Close-ratio gearbox, 49–50
Coil ignition, 40
Coil spring, 53
Concentric carburettor, 23
Constant-mesh gearbox, 49
Contact-breaker-less ignition, 41
Cubic capacity, 18
Damping mechanism, 62
Desmodromic designs, 13
Diaphragm spring, 53
Disc brakes, 58

Eastern European machines, 8
Electric machines, 11, 22
Electric starter, 44
Electrical systems, 69
Energy transfer ignition, 40
Engines, 11
    electric, 18, 22
    four-cylinder, 18, 21–22
    four-stroke, 11–14
    measurement, 18
    noise, 36
    overhead-camshaft, 13
    single-cylinder, 18
    three-cylinder, 18

Engines, *(Cont.)*
    twin-cylinder, 18, 19
    two-stroke, 13—14
    Wankel, 12
Excise duty, 91—92
Exhaust emissions, 14

Face masks, 101—102
Fairings, 104
Four-cylinder engine, 18, 21—22
Four-stroke engine, 11—14
Front suspension, 61
Fuel economy, 33
Fuel injection, 23
Fully-comprehensive insurance, 92

Gauntlets, 102—103
Gearboxes, 47
    automatic, 54
    close-ratio, 49—50
    constant-mesh, 49
    standard-ratio, 49—50
    unit-construction, 48—49
    wide-ratio, 49—50
Gloves, 102—103
Goggles, 102
Grass-track racing, 107
Greasing, 73
Greeves, 9

Handlebars, 67
    racing type, 67
    chopper type, 67—68
Headstock spindle adjustment, 66
Helmets, 101
Hydraulic brakes, 58

Ignition advance, 41
Ignition systems, 39
    coil ignition, 40—41
    contact-breaker-less, 41
    energy transfer, 40
    magneto, 39
    transistorised, 43
Ignition timing, 78
Insurance, 92 et seq
    fully-comprehensive, 92
    thrid-party, 92

Japanese design, 7

Kick starter, 44, 45

Learning to ride, 96
Licensing, 90 et seq
    provisional licence, 90
    tests, 90—91
Lights, 69—71
Luggage carriers, 104

Machines, types of, 1 et seq
Magnesium wheels, 59
Magneto ignition, 39
Maintenance, 72 et seq
    tools, 80—83
Monobloc carburettor, 26
Mopeds, 2—4
    electric, 22
M.O.T. tests, 93
Motor-cycle design, 6—7
    Japanese, 7
Multi-cylinder designs, 21
Multi-plate clutch, 51

Non-butted spokes, 60

Oil-metering system, 14—16
Overhead-camshaft engine, 13

Panniers, 104
Performance figures, 4
Primary-chain adjustment, 48
Provisional licence, 90
Purchasing a machine, 4—6
Push starting, 46

Rear suspension, 61, 64
Re-boring, 87—89
Riding equipment, 99
    boots, 102
    face masks, 101—102
    gauntlets, 102—103
    goggles, 102
    helmets, 101
    safety bars, 103
    suits, 100
Riding suits, 100
Road racing, 107

Safety bars, 103
Safety helmets, 95, 101
Scrambling, 107
Shaft-drive, 54, 55
Shoe-and-drum brake, 56
Sidecars, 9—10, 97 et seq
Single-cylinder engine, 18
Slide-operated-throttle carburettor, 32—33
Spanners, 82—83
Spokes, 59, 60
Sporting activity, 105
    grass-track racing, 107
    road-racing, 107
    scrambling, 107
    trials, 106—107
Springs
    coil, 53
    diaphragm, 53
Standard-ratio gearbox, 49—50
Spot lamps, 104—105
Starting, 43
    electric starter, 44—45
    kick starter, 44, 45
    push starting, 46
Steering, 65 et seq
SU carburettors, 35
Suspension, 61
    adjustment, 64—65
    damping mechanism, 62
    front, 61
    purpose of, 61
    rear, 61, 64

Third-party insurance, 92
Three-cylinder engine, 19—20
Throttle-stop screw, 27—28
Transistorised ignition, 41—43
Trials, 106
Trouble shooting, 83 et seq
Twin-cylinder engine, 19—20
Tyres, 60
    pressure, 61
    wear, 60—61

Unit-construction gearbox, 48—49

Vacuum carburettor, 34—35

Wankel engine, 12
Water cooling, 22
Wheel alignment, 67
Wheels, 59
    magnesium, 59
    spokes, 59
    truing, 59
Wide-ratio gearbox, 49—50

How? What? Where? Why?

These little books have all the answers

for more details please write to

 Newnes Technical Books

Butterworths, Borough Green, Sevenoaks, Kent TN15 8PH

Questions and Answers

J N Seale

DIESEL ENGINES

Designed to present to the operating engineer and to students of diesel engines a clear and reliable account of principles and practice of the whole range of diesel engine operation, from the high speed industrial unit to the largest multi-horsepower marine engine. This latest reprint is in SI (metric) units where applicable.

CONTENTS: Principles of Operation, Engine Types and Application, Starting Methods, Fuel-Injection Pumps, Governors, Fuel Injectors, Fuel Filters, Useful Units and Metric Conversion Factors, Index.

128 pages   1964   0 600 41254 7

Newnes Technical Books

Butterworths, Borough Green, Sevenoaks, Kent TN15 8PH

Questions & Answers
Automobile Transmission Systems
E B Weston

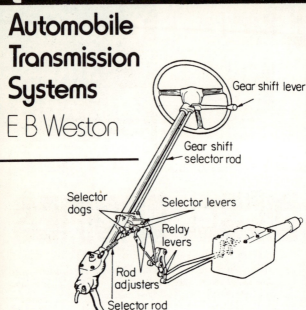

With the aid of simple diagrams and concise answers to the many questions which puzzle the beginner and student this book leads the reader, step by step, to a useful level of practical knowledge

160 pages   1976   0 408 00184 4

For more details of the book and many others please write to

 Newnes Technical Books

Butterworths, Borough Green, Sevenoaks, Kent